T0146465

Why You Should Forgive Others

Why You Should Forgive Others

Susan Sykes

iUniverse

WHY YOU SHOULD FORGIVE OTHERS

iUniverse books may be ordered through booksellers or by contacting:

iUniverse
1663 Liberty Drive
Bloomington, IN 47403
www.iuniverse.com
1-800-Authors (1-800-288-4677)

ISBN: 978-1-5320-4014-6 (sc)
ISBN: 978-1-5320-4015-3 (e)

Library of Congress Control Number: 2018902993

Scripture quotations taken from the 21st Century King James Version®, copyright © 1994. Used by permission of Deuel Enterprises, Inc., Gary, SD 57237. All rights reserved.

Scripture taken from the New King James Version®. Copyright © 1982 by Thomas Nelson. Used by permission. All rights reserved.

Print information available on the last page.

iUniverse rev. date: 05/10/2019

Contents

Scriptures to Read

1 Peter 4:8, And above all things have fervent love for one another, for love will cover a multitude of sins.

1 Peter 5:7, casting all your care upon Him, for he cares for you.

John 10:27, My Sheep hear my voice and I know them and they follow Me.

1 John 4:7-8, Beloved let us love one another, for love is of God; and everyone who loves is born of God and knows God. He who does not love does not know God, for God is love.

1 John 4:18-19, There is no fear in love; but perfect love cast out fear, because fear involves torment, but he who fears has not been made perfect in love. We love, him because he first loved us.

1 John 1:6, if we say that we have fellowship with Him and walk in darkness, we lie and do not practice the truth.

Ephesians 3:17 that Christ may dwell in your hearts through faith; that you, "being rooted and grounded in love.

Ephesians 4:32, and be kind to one another tenderhearted, "forgiving one another, even as God in Christ forgave you.

Ephesians 5:17 Therefore do not be unwise, but understand what the will of the Lord is.

Psalms 51:10 Create in me a clean heart, o God, and renew a steadfast spirit within me.

Psalm 55:19 God will hear and afflict them, "even he who abides from of old. Because they do not change, therefore they do not fear God.

James 4:17 therefore, "to him who knows, to do Good, and does not do it, to him it is sin.

Roman 7:20 Now if I do what I will not to do, it is no longer I who do it, but sin that dwells in me.

Roman 8:6 for to be carnally minded is death, but to be spiritually minded is life and peace.

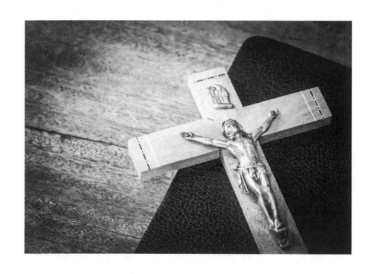

Dedication

I would like to dedicate this book to my Lord and Savior Jesus Christ. I want to thank Him for keeping me for all these years of my life and renewing the right spirit in me. Since Jesus came into my life, I'm a much better person and my life has been changed. Secondly, I want to thank all of the churches I attended. The first church I attended once I became an adult and realized I needed Jesus Christ was Bethel AME Church—Dr. Frank M. Reid III, Evangel Cathedral Upper Marlboro, MD—Bishop Don Mears, Victory Church—Dr. Gary V. Whetstone, The Living Word Church, Greater Victory and Deliverance Church—Pastor Douglas and Mrs. Phillips First Lady, Salt Nation Church—Bishop Kenyan and last my MBCS Bible College. I want to thank you all for teaching the Word of God and being faithful. It help me mature in Jesus Christ. Christ nature, ways and agape kind of love. Thanks again to all and the church families.

Next, I dedicate this book to my husband, my children, all family members, friends, and many others. You are not alone, my heart and prayers goes out to you all. I pray you find some kind of truth, love and victory in your heart from this book.

Introduction

MY PURPOSE OF WRITING this book, is to help as many marriages, as I can. When your marriage begin to fail and divorce is stepping in. There is a way to work the marriage out but only through the Blood of Jesus Christ and His love. What God put together let no person on this earth come in between the two. It might look impossible for the marriage to be fixed but with God all things are possible. If you really want it to work out, never give up or give in. Both partners need to work as one because marriage is hard work sometimes. You are not alone.

I also want to help reach the lost souls. People that are in relationships, single mom and dad, marriage partners who are separated, for every couple, people who want to be married, single men, single women, as well as young and old. People that don't know our Lord and Savior. Everyone who have been hurt, in pain, stressed, bitter and depressed by others that we truly love. There is a way out of bondage, darkness, and heartaches. We have to keep a clear mind and think positive, while moving forward in life. Relationships can leave scars and pain, but thank God, who can heal and deliver.

Remember where the trust has been broken and you can't see your way through, Jesus is the answer to all our problems and situations. Build your love one up by showing love, be gentle, kind, have self-control, forgive and make peace. Do unto the spouse, what you would have them do for you. Pray, forgive, plead the Blood of Jesus and let nothing tear your marriage apart. All things are possible but you both have to put in the time, the effect and hard work. I'm sorry if things are not, what they should be but my heart and prayers goes out to you all. You are not alone.

Definitions

Apologize—to say you are sorry for something

Arrogant—considering yourself more important than others

Bible—book of life, our basic instruction before leaving the earth

Build—the shape and size of a person body

Caring—to think something is important or interesting; to feel concerned about something

Curse—a spell intended to bring harm or bad luck to somebody

Encourage—to give somebody the confidence to do something

Give—to bend or break, to hand something over to someone else

Give in—to finally agree to something that you do not want to do

Hard to forgive—just can't forgive

Harm—to hurt or damage

Hatred—to dislike very much, a strong dislike

Hurt—to cause pain or unhappiness

Kindness—friendly and good to others, kind

Love—to care for somebody or something very much, lovable. A strong feeling of liking somebody

Meek—quiet, gentle, and obedient

Patient—the ability to be patient, wait, able to wait a long time

Peace—a time when there is no war, quiet and calm

Power—strength or force, the ability to do something

Rude—bad mannered; not polite

Sharing—to divide something among several people

Stop—to put off doing something

Unforgiving—not allowing for error or shortcoming, especially in being harsh, an unforgiving person

Wendy Black Life Story, Childhood to Adulthood

WENDY WAS BORN IN Georgia, in a green house, in the country. Back in the 1960's when she was born they had mid wives, to help deliver a child. The towns were small, where everyone knew each other. No buses ran in the area, no hospitals near and no stores close by. You needed a car to get around on the long dirt roads. Her mom was married to her dad William, there are three children now. At night it was very dark and a few people had outdoor bathrooms, meaning they had to go outside to go to the bathroom. They had a big yard, garden full of fruit and vegetables. The stores and schools were a distance away from their home. People walked for miles to get school, even in the snow, rain and heat. There wasn't much to do down there but go to church, a few parties, work and drink. They grew weed and made moon shine liquor in the woods, especially on the weekend or Sunday, when the liquor store was closed. People would see who had the booze.

One day William was drinking, and a man was getting fresh with Wendy's mother. Her dad went all the way home, got his gun and came back, he shot the man. He ended up in jail for some years and Wendy's mom started dating someone else a few years later. Later they moved away, while the father was still in jail. When William got out of jail and realized they were gone he began to date a woman. Her name was Debbie and she had four daughters already. After 6 years Debbie had another girl by Mr. William and she looked like Wendy. They could have gone for twins. Wendy's dad and mom got a divorce because his girlfriend told him to, so he did. Wendy, her sister and brother, were unable to see their dad for some years.

Wendy's mother (Karen), ended up with a set of twin boys, by one of her sister's husband. Ms. Karen was very sorry for that mistake because she hurt her own sister, who she loved. In the country, everyone just about knew each other, or people were related in some kind of way. Her sister was very mad at Wendy's mom but the temptation was very strong in those days and still is today, 2017. Karen and her sister were not speaking for about one year but they knew things would come back right. Their mom had passed away, when they were small kids. They never had a chance to really love their mom or know her. They were unable to talk to their mom, share stories, and had no role model as a mother. Never got a chance to experience a mother and daughter relationship like other people did. Wendy's mother still to this day cries, has bad feelings in her heart because she was unable to share her love with the one who helped bring her into this world. She was just a child barely walking. Ms. Karen does have a very good relationship with all her daughters, but she thinks about her mother and feels the emptiness on Mother's Day for her mom. Something she missed out on, while growing up. She made a big mistake by betraying her sister. They knew how to stick together no matter what had happen because their life wasn't easy growing up without their mom and dad. Their dad was there for a little while after Wendy's grandmother passed away, but he also passed a little while later. Wendy's mom, Karen, was a small child when their parents died, and they were sent to the grandmother but she was old and passed away, also. Next it was other people in the family taking care of them, so Wendy's mom lived a poor life. After Wendy's mom had the twin boys, she met a very kind man about twelve months later and they begin having an affair. One year later the children moved with their mother and the boyfriend to another state and that is where they stayed for some years, until he got abusive and wanted to put his hands on Wendy's mother. But there were also plenty of happy moments and family time.

Wendy remembered in the 1960's-1970's how they used to play in the woods. There was a lady named Gertrude, who was always in the woods and carrying bags. The children would make her chase them by picking at the lady. The lady looked spooky, had thick dusty short hair, her eyes glowed in the dark and she walked with a big black cane. One day they said, "Hey you can't get us"! Ms. Gertrude turned around and said, "Oh yes I can". All the kids began to run from her, as the lady ran behind them shaking her cane and shouting, "I'm going to get you". The kids were scared and ran all the way home. They thought it was fun. In those days, children also used to make money by picking nuts up off the ground, put them in a bag and get them weighted at a warehouse. You were able to take empty soda bottles and get money for those too. Wendy had trees in the back of their house, and in different areas around the town where they picked blue berries, and strawberries off the tree and ate them. There were apple trees in the back of their house too, some apples would be on the ground or they would climb the tree and get some apples to eat. Wendy and the other kids used to build a play house out of big boxes. They played mommy and daddy, played marbles, hop scotch, jump rope the double-dutch, and hide-go-seek. Other games were red light and green light, mother may I, went skating in the street, played tag, freeze tag, blind man's bluff, heads up, jacks, marbles, Simon says, Double Dutch jump rope and Musical chairs. Those were the good old days.

Children respected their elders, parents, teachers, and other adults. If you used bad language you would get your lips snapped and sometimes it might be bleeding. Being disrespectful got children plenty of beatings, from neighbors and both parents. There was less violence, not much bullying, they respected the teachers, sat in their seat and did their work in school. The kids played together well, not a lot of guns for children to get easily, and everyone enjoyed life. Parents would use switches (tree branches) on a kid, for being a hard head or they used a cord. They lit a child's butt's up, spanked the bottom really hard, when a kid got out of control or rude to an adult. People tried not to use switches and cords too much because it could leave scars on the children, might even kill them. They wanted them to know they meant business when they told them what to do and what not to do. The music back in the old days had real true meaning, great love songs, songs that touch the heart and might make you cry. It was much safer living in those days and people could even leave their doors unlocked. The world has totally changed. Where did all the love go for one another? God wants us all to love everyone and make amends to whoever you are holding grudges against, your family, neighbors, church members, and persons of different races, friends, and especially your parents. No one is perfect. Children and parents found ways to forgive. God sees our heart and knows us all. Are your ways pleasing to our Lord and Savior?

Wendy remembers the bell bottom pants, high heel shoes, afro hair style and the dirt roads. There was a funeral home in the complex in the place where they used to live. The children played in the funeral home a lot. Many people ran out of there straight through the glass door when they went to view a loved one's dead body. They had to get that door fix so many times. Many times there were bats that got into Wendy's house, they would be behind the curtains in the living room. They would be sitting in the living room watching TV when all of a sudden, a shadow would pop up, flying from one side of the window to the other side. The children would start to scream and run into one of the bedrooms and close the door. When they did that, it made it hard for them to figure out where the bat went. They would open the bedroom door and peek, walk slow and quiet, trying to find the bat. The next thing they knew the bat would begin flying through the house. Wendy and the family would hit at it with a broom or anything they could find until it was dead. That was not fun at all. One night, the bats came out of nowhere and people were outside playing, having a nice summer evening, when bundles of bats appeared. Some people were yelling, running in the house while others were hitting at them. It was like a nightmare or a movie where bats attack people. Wendy hated that and was glad when they moved away. Bats always got in the house and it was scary.

Everything was going well. Wendy's mom always sent the kids to church, but Ms. Karen and her boyfriend never went. They should have gone to church with the children. Her mother

(Ms. Karen), was a short light skinned lady and her bruises showed really good on her skin. The man was real nice to the children but sometimes would beat the mom when he got drunk. He put his hands on Karen about two or three times. The children were small, and they would just listen while the mom would cry. As soon as the boyfriend would leave the room, the kids ran into the room to their mom. They told their mom to call her sisters and she did. One time they all left him but came back and he tried to be nice for a minute but later hit her for the last time. Wendy, her sisters and brothers even though they were small, stood up for their mom. This time when they called the mom's sisters, they warned him not to touch Karen anymore and that they would be down there. They sent money for the second time for plane tickets so Ms. Karen and the kids could come to Atlanta, Georgia. The family never went back again and was set free from the violence. Her mom did have twin girls by him, she was pregnant when they left him for the last time and came back to Atlanta. Twins ran in the family, in fact Karen's birth mom miscarried about three sets of twins, before she had the last five children. Ms. Karen and all her children ended up being separated. They were divided between Ms. Karen's two sisters.

Wendy was the oldest girl, so her and all her sisters stayed with one aunt and all her brothers stayed with the mother (Karen) and the other aunt. Wendy said that the aunt they stayed with was the mean one. Sometimes one of the girls would pee the bed and the aunt would beat her tail because the bathroom was right there in the room. All you had to do was actually roll over and the bathroom door was staring you right in your face. Wendy and her sisters knew if one peed in the bed, they all would get in trouble because they started blaming one another. The aunt would beat all of them. The aunt would smell the pee and make them get out the bed and check the kids. The kids would even try to fan themselves and the wet spot on the bed,.hoping everything would be dry before the aunt woke up. What a miserable feeling, getting a beating and your mom was separated from you. They couldn't wait to get out of that house. It wasn't long before Wendy's mom found a place to live. About three years later down the road their mom found another male friend. She took her time before dating again.

After being abused Ms. Karen, never took stuff from another man again. She would let them know that if they put their hands on her they would be out of her house in a second. She took good care of all her children and her children always came first in her life. Wendy, her sisters and her brothers made sure no other man put their hands on their mother. Karen had six kids and two were sets of twin boys and girls. Wendy's mother got a job and was doing well. She never talked bad about any of the children's fathers. The abusive boyfriend came to Atlanta to see the twin girls twice and never again.

Wendy's mom worked and took care of all of the kids without any child support. She did have a little help from Social

Services but once the kids got in middle school, they worked as well. Wendy and the other children were able to buy their own school clothes by working the summer Jobs Corp. They loved their mother and she loved them. Karen never held a grudge or had an unforgiving spirit toward the men in her life. Wendy's mom and her mother's sisters are all still together, loving each other and if anything they always got rid of the men in their life and kept the relationship with each other.

They are older today and still the whole family is loving, strong, even the children. Their mom did a good job taking care of them; she refused to complain and always kept striving toward the future. She had a meek and humble attitude. Never complained or blamed the absent parent because we all have made mistakes in our lives. No one is perfect but we can change our ways and learn from our mistakes. Leave the past behind and keep peace toward all people, no matter what you have been through. You are not alone.

Wendy Black: First Boyfriend

NOW WENDY'S MOM AND all the kids are in their new home in Atlanta. The children are so glad they are with their mother (Karen). It was like a nightmare, living with someone else, even though it was a relative. Sometimes the family can be annoying. The children also went to church sometimes with their other aunt and her children. When they were in church it felt like hours and after service the aunt would talk with other members in the church for hours. It was fun going to church and seeing the people dancing and falling all over the place, having the Holy Ghost.

At the present time, Wendy knew going to church was a good thing because she went before she ever came to Atlanta. Considering the fact that she still didn't understand much about the Word of God, but she still went to church. The Word of God did draw her attention, because there is no man on this earth that could build or create the Heavens, moon, stars, sun, rain, snow, hail, lightning, thunder, oceans, sea, clouds. It has to be someone with higher power which is God. There is no one who can do the things God can do. It is impossible for man to do these things. Wendy wasn't able to understand her purpose for being here on this earth, not yet.

She met her first boyfriend, while in middle school. He was brown skinned, chocolate and bow legged and two years older than her. His name, was Alex and he seemed kind of shy. Wendy was a little shy also. After school a few of the kids would go and hang out in the alley, near the back of Wendy's house. There was a wall they would sit on, and drink, smoke, talk, listen to music, watch people walk up and down the street, until it got dark. Alex was a person who carried one of those big loud boom box radios and they would begin jamming.

People always had house parties on the weekends. Everyone would check them out and see which ones were jamming. The basement would be full of smoke, unless the parents said no smoking but those were the best days and less killing. Now you have to watch your surroundings carefully and avoid too many crowds.

The other wall where everyone hung out had train tracks at the other end of the alley. They played on the tracks and in the woods. Years ago you could leave your doors unlocked but not anymore. Everyone got along much better, had respect for one another, especially for the adults or the elderly.

One night when Alex was sitting on the wall and Wendy was walking home or leaving home going over to her girlfriend's house, he wished on a falling star that she would be his girlfriend one day. One day they started talking. His wish on the falling star came true. Wendy went to his house one day. In the basement they played some music. The guys in those days were able to have company in the basement and their parents allowed them to have their freedom. The parents came down stairs only to wash clothes, unless they needed something else from down there. Wendy and Alex would slow dance, getting to know each other and drawing near. Later they fell in love and were with each other daily. A few years later, she would stay the night only sometimes because Alex also had to share the basement with his brother. His brother also brought his girlfriends over and sometimes they would stay the night. Those were the good old times with less crimes. They did a lot of walking, while jamming with the big boom box. There were no cell phones but only house phones. When you saw Alex, you saw Wendy. One day, she went down to Alex's house looking for him but he wasn't home yet. Alex's father said, "Are you looking for your other half"?

She said, "Yes".

He said, "I'll let him know that you came by".

They were so in love and did many things together. One day they went to a store and some of the older men were outside the store just standing around. One of the men said, "How do you ugly guys get all the pretty women"?

Alex and Wendy just laughed, they were just playing but

on the other hand they might be serious. Alex wasn't all that but he wasn't bad looking either. What got Wendy's attention was his personality, his walk, gentleness, and smile. That was what mattered to her and what drew her to him. He was her chocolate bunny. She had actually thought if they ever broke up, she didn't know what she would do without him. And that the world was going to come to an end. In marriage and relationships when one person gets hurt, especially the ladies, it feels like someone ripped your heart out, or just threw it away and stepped on it. It made you feel less than a woman or what did I do to deserve this?

At this time in her life death was scary and she wanted to be with him forever. Most people think the same thing today and don't want to be alone. That is because when you love someone, treated them nice, fell in love, gave your all to them and they stepped out on you, it truly hurts. Since this lady has been with Alex, she hadn't been attending church anymore and he never went. Wendy does know that God exists but still is a babe in Christ.

Things were going fine between the couple until high school. She was two years younger than Alex and she was now in high school. Sometimes she would stop by Alex's class to talk to him. Everyone in the class would look to see who it was at the door, even the girls. Eventually Alex got a car in the 12th grade and was working. The girls in his class started to like him and that's when problems started to rise.

Time went on and the young couple had a car to ride in. It was much faster and easier to get around in a car. They spent most of their time together on the weekend and sometime through the week.

When Alex got out of school, Wendy still had two more years to go. He worked and she also worked while in middle school and high school. Her first real job was working with her mother and one of her sisters as a waitress in a restaurant. She couldn't serve alcoholic drinks because she was too young. The men loved seeing Wendy in the restaurant because she never wore makeup. They thought she was cute with her natural face and one of the men called her bright eyes.

Wendy bought clothes for her and Alex sometimes so they both could look good together and wear the same color. They were together most of the time. When you saw Wendy, they were either together or her man was not far behind.

Alex's cheating started and one of her sisters saw him out at the park a few times with another girl but never told Wendy. She was mad at him because one night, she went over to his house on a Friday and he never came home until about three o'clock in the morning. His parents were up in age and had taken a vacation that week but the basement door was unlocked. Back then you were able to leave the doors unlocked and feel safe in your home.

His brother went to pick some girl up, and it wasn't his main lady. Wendy heard them come in and went upstairs to hide. After they did what they did, Alex's brother took the girl home. She wanted to boil water on the stove for Alex but the brother came back too fast. She grabbed a knife and ran upstairs to the third floor. She was very high from drinking all day and had no clue where Alex was. Wendy always would walk the streets late at night looking and waiting until he came home because they were always together.

The things we do for love sometimes is disheartening. She wouldn't walk the streets late by herself now, as you can see love can make a person do some crazy things. But they were young and learning, we all make or have made mistakes. No one is perfect and you learn from your mistakes. Love shouldn't hurt, it is caring for one another it's about honoring it, respecting your one and only true love.

This night he and one of his buddies drove up to the house and parked the car. They were sitting in the car feeling up this girl and kissing her. Wendy was looking out the window at them and couldn't believe what she was seeing. Her heart was beating fast and she was hurting on the inside. Alex had to be feeling good this night because this is not the first time Wendy was waiting for him. He should have known better. He knew they only lived about two minutes away from each other. They were so high and were feeling up the girl and they all were sitting in the front seat together. They got out of the car laughing and they all went upstairs and got butt naked in the small room. Wendy was hot and mad. She saw Alex's buddy go first and when Alex joined in, Wendy wanted to throw hot boiling water on them. She had the knife, walked in on them and just started swinging. She cut Alex on the shoulder, his brother ran upstairs and threw Wendy out. The brother told Alex to call the police but he refused to.

Wendy went home crying and upset, she went back and damaged the brother's car that night because he allowed them to continue to do what they were doing and he might have joined them. When morning came, the brother was at Wendy's door, trying to get to her. He threw big bricks at her mother's door; he was mad. They had to call the police on him in order for him to leave their house.

A few days later Alex came up to Wendy's house to apologize but she was still hurt and crying. Alex said, "There was nothing else he could do but to say he was sorry. Try to think before acting out because some things are not worth you going to jail".

Wendy's graduation from 12th grade was coming up in two days. Alex wasn't going to come because Wendy was still not talking to him. Her sister saw him with a different lady again out in the park. This time she told Wendy. Wendy felt so bad and disappointed but her and her family went on to the graduation. She had called Alex and he said he would be there and he did show up. But the trust was broken and the relationship wasn't as strong anymore. It was a painful relationship from now on. It was pay back and revenge time because of so much pain. Two wrongs really don't make things better or right, but when a person is not grounded in the Word of God, the ways of a man seem right but the wager of sin is death.

Wendy started to have male friends that she would see when they were on bad times. It was time for a change in her life. When you see yourself going through the same stuff, try making changes in your mind. One day, Alex was looking for her and she was with Kevin. Alex had an idea where the young man lived so he was riding around in the area and that day Kevin was walking her home. When they saw the car, Alex jumped out and wanted to fight. Kevin was telling Alex to leave Wendy alone because she can do what she wanted to and he couldn't stop her. Alex was chasing Kevin around the car and Wendy left but Alex caught up with her before she got home. Men hate when the tables turn and you start seeing someone. They think it is only ok for them to fool around. They can get their feelings hurt also. He jumped out of his car arguing with her. He hit her so hard, she fell to the ground. Some men in a car riding by told him to not hit her anymore.

She was able to get up and go home; she was almost at the house. The couple didn't live far from each other, just down the street and around the corner. Temptation is very real and is strong, and will bring a person down if you let it. Things were not getting much better because they were both trying to get even with one another. Later they would make up and things would be alright for a while but it was the things they were doing while apart and mad at each other, that they both got other people's phone numbers and talked to other people but they still loved and cared for each other. The game was still being played but both tried to be careful and not get caught. They both knew if they couldn't find their other half, they were with someone else. Two wrongs don't make things right, especially not in a marriage because most of the time, it gets worse.

There is a thin line between love and hate; once you love them then you hate them. That is a game for fools. The games that some people play, how many of us have friends you can truly trust? Alex and Wendy tried to hang in there and show their love for each other a little longer. Alex got caught a few more times with other women. Wendy continued to play around and try to be strong. When doing harm to each other, a person only hurts themself and makes it harder to forgive one another. That was her first love and it was hard to let go. You can sleep around, play around but what it all boils down to is that you are still in love, are hurting, and you want to be with that one true love. People are still hurting because the one you thought cared for you, made a fool out of you and it hurts. Wendy would see Alex's car while on the bus riding by, either she was going home or leaving home. She would get off the bus and knock on the doors, until it was the right one and he would come out and leave with her. Or Alex always got caught by bringing the woman to his mother's house because Wendy would be waiting.

One day she got tired of waiting, it was late but she did go back early that morning. Alex had brought a lady friend home with him. She was right there in the living room because he was getting ready to take her home. The father answered the door and Wendy walked in, he was busted. He told Wendy, they had gone out and she couldn't get in her house. She kindly rode with him to take her home; this lady thought Wendy was going to get in the back seat of the car, but Wendy said to her,"You get in the back," and she did. Alex dropped her off around the corner from her house not in the front.

One day, Wendy and her best friend went around the area, trying to see where the girl lived. They found it, she was sitting outside in the front of her house with her boyfriend. Wendy and her lady friend walked up and told her boyfriend that last night his lady stayed at her boyfriend's house. Then they left and the two begin arguing. Love can make you do crazy things but is that real love? The world is full of games and people get hurt all the time but that is how it is.

A year later, Wendy and Alex moved together. Wendy was working down the harbor and Alex would pick her up most of the time and if he didn't he was up to no good. They were still trying to make it work. They had a nice little place in the county, with two bed-rooms. Her uncle had co-signed for her and they ended up breaking the lease. What happened was Wendy realized that Alex was still being unfaithful in so many ways.

One night, she had a talk with Alex and said how she hoped that he didn't get anyone pregnant while they were together. He told her that he wouldn't do that. A few nights later, Alex was high and told her someone was pregnant by him and Wendy was in shock. She asked, "Why, how many months and how long was he seeing her"?

He said, she was eight months, so she was getting ready to have the baby. Alex told her everything and where she lived. Wendy and one of her other girlfriends went to the woman's house but didn't let Alex know. She met the lady and they talked. There was nothing anyone could do about the situation because she was going to have her child no matter what. Wendy was very frustrated with the situation but it shouldn't have been a big surprise, the way the relationship had been going.

She was hurt, one Tuesday morning Alex was at work and all she could do was cry and cry, and drink, as she thought about all she had been through with Alex, all the pain, the stress, hardened heart and suffering in her life. She was cleaning up the apartment and washing dishes, while she was doing the dishes, she put her hand in the glass and the glass cracked and cut her finger. It was bleeding real bad and wouldn't stop. She ran up the street to the store to get a bandage, you could see the white meat lift up on the finger.

Wendy was scared and didn't want to go to the Emergency Room.

When she got to work the next day, she took the bandage off. Her co-worker helped her when she pulled the bandage off. The white meat lifted up and it hurt. They told Wendy to go to the hospital, she went and the doctor told her it was good that she came because if she had waited too much longer, they would have had to cut her finger off. The doctor had to put stitches on the inside and outside of the finger. Until this day, she avoided using glasses to drink out of, she had a few glasses for company but she used plastic cups or hard mugs.

Be careful who you want to share your life with because you can live miserable or be happy. Love is blind sometimes, wake up. People are going to only do what we allow them to do to us. Wendy had a big decision to make and it was not easy. She decided, to go to her aunt for help and attend church with her again but the aunt stopped going to church and said there was no God. But Wendy knew better than that because God created this world. Wendy just didn't have enough knowledge about God but knew he was real and knew his name. People suffered because of a lack of knowledge of Christ. They don't have a clue why things happen the way they do. Her aunt's statement about Christ kept Wendy away from God much longer because now she was confused. Satan enjoyed playing tricks with everyone's mind. Her and Alex got evicted and moved back home with their parents.

A few month later, they moved in with one of Alex's sisters' house. The baby was born and Wendy wanted to plot a conspiracy against Alex, because she never tried to tie them down by having kids, and she really loved him. He was her first love and when you love a person it is not that easy to walk away. She had to think about the conspiracy, her life, his child without a dad, and was it worth killing for. The answer, was no, it's not worth taking someone's life because your life would also be over living behind bars for the rest of your life. It's called think before you react because the consequences are horrible. She really didn't want to harm Alex because her love for him was like heaven.

Wendy had enough now and needed to leave the relationship. If you are not married you have a chance to get out of a miserable relationship and make a change in your life. You deserve to be treated as a queen. The last thing that happened was when Alex came home high at his sister's place and it was late. Wendy was in the bed; he got in the bed and was making crazy sounds and shaking. She had no idea what kind of drug he used. Wendy was scared, she put her clothes on and left the house. As she was leaving, a thought occurred to her, what if something happened to him or he died? People might think she had something to do with it, but he was ok.

The next morning the police went with Wendy and got all her belongings out. Alex's sister asked her why she had called the police. Alex's sister said, you could have got all your things out without the police". The police asked her how long were the couple together? She said, "About eight years or longer". The police told Wendy she should consider marriage and that she didn't have to leave.

But it was over and she left. She forgave him, still cared for him and saw him sometimes. He started really using but he was already on something. Wendy didn't know much about these drugs people were on. She knew she didn't want any after seeing Alex's reaction to the drugs. They were young and were experiencing life, relationships, like others, looking for love in all the wrong places. Without Jesus Christ in your relationship, you will go through things in your life which will, eventually lead you to Him. No matter how bad the pain may be, forgive and move on. Forgive everyone who have hurt you, just like Christ forgave us for our sins. We all have made mistakes in our life but you are not alone. Make wise decisions, think positive in the mind and let go of the past strongholds in your life. Alex was in Wendy's second relationship for a minute but not long. He was mad because she had found someone else years later but Wendy's family still liked Alex. Alex wanted to fight Wendy's new boyfriend.

Alex was still visiting, Wendy's family before he passed away. He told many people that he was going to marry Wendy and she was the only one he truly loved. People if you have a good person in your life, hold on, put Jesus Christ in your relationship because people don't realize what they have until the well runs dry. You don't have to get revenge or get even just leave them in God's hands and continue to pray for the loved one. We can't change any one, only God can make a difference in people's lives. You can also sow or plant a seed in their heart. Which is the word of God.

Wendy Black 2nd Relationship

WENDY TOOK HER TIME before, starting a new relationship. She had to get over her feelings for Alex, her first love. Ms. Black had no kids, went to work and was enjoying her life, with family members and friends. She wasn't trying to date.

After months went by, she stayed at one of her girl cousin's house. She tried not to think about Alex and was doing great. One day, she was on the porch on a cloudy Saturday afternoon and a gentlemen walked by. He must have been going to work. Wendy said hello to the man as he continued walking.

The next time she saw him she stopped him and asked, "Where are you going"? He said. "To work". They were talking for a little while and she got his phone number. He was some kin to Wendy's brother's girlfriend, and they lived around the corner. Ms. Black watched him as he walked down the street.

They started dating and became close. It still didn't dawn on her to seek Jesus Christ and His ways. The relationship began, and John was happy. Wendy walked around to his aunt's house and they was teasing him because he had a girlfriend. Later he started staying with Wendy, at her cousin's place. Wendy's boy cousin saw John leave the house one day. He asked, "Girl what did you do to that boy? He was smiling from ear to ear!"

Wendy said, "I didn't do anything!" He was a nice person, had no kids, never married and had served in the military. He wore dress clothes so Wendy, didn't have to dress him. He was a very neat and clean, young man.

They stayed with Wendy's cousin for about six months in the city. Then they moved back home with their parents to save money. John had to catch the bus, from across town from his mom's house to her mom's house to visit her. She was pregnant by John. Alex was still friends with the family and hung out sometimes with Wendy's brother Sly. Alex came down to her mom's house one day and didn't know she was pregnant. Oh that hurt him to his heart but remember Alex had a child in their relationship. Ms. Black was having a child but she wasn't with him anymore. Alex tried to pick a fight with John in her mother's house. Her mother liked Alex and asked what was going on downstairs in the kitchen? One of her sisters, said Alex was trying to start a fight and that he was high. Wendy's brother came down and they left the house. You could tell Alex was doing drugs, that was her heart but now she had John. She now had a new love, and was going to have John's child. She did talk to Alex every once in a while even though they were not together.

Alex was messing with one of the girls where her mother lived who was doing drugs too. One day Ms. Black called Alex and the girl answered the phone. The girls begin to argue but Wendy didn't worry because they weren't together. Alex did come back down to the house a few more times with Wendy's brother. Wendy and John moved out of their parents' house and got their own place in the country. It was a town house with two bedrooms, and a basement with a washer and dryer. She had her first child, a boy, and was happy.

The couple stayed at his place for one year and somehow, John started acting wilder. He wasn't working at his job anymore, wanted to sell vacuum cleaners and other products. She didn't understand this drug thing and knew nothing about it or how powerful it was. John's father co-signed to help John get a car. It was a probe car, white and pretty. John started to work later and was hyper (couldn't be still), he kept running in and out of the house. Going around the corner with one of his buddies who didn't work but his buddy's children's mother worked. His buddy had plenty of kids. John's buddy, would just get high all day and John would go join him. You become who you hang around with. If you hung around with positive people you have a better chance of becoming a successful person. Being around negative people, you stay negative. People can change with the help of God if they truly want to. John was slipping away and not realizing he was headed in the wrong direction. Wendy Black had no problem with him cheating or if he did she never knew or he gave her no idea he was.

John began to act different. It was a Sunday morning, John went out and came home later. He would go into the bathroom and stay a long time. Ms. Black would ask, "What are you doing"? He was in there getting high but never would let her see what he was using. Plus she had the baby boy. They went downstairs to the kitchen and John was still smoking and whatever else he was doing. He started staring and looking out the window, saying the police were outside, he couldn't keep still and was paranoid. Wendy was looking at him, thinking, he is losing his mind.

She said to John, "Let me try some". He said, "No". She just wanted to see what he was going to say. But she was glad he said no because who wants to live like that, paranoid and hooked on something so powerful.

Wendy just couldn't believe her eyes to see how his life was changing to something worse. He kept looking out the window thinking he was hearing sounds. John started going out of town and not coming home for days. Left Wendy and the baby home, without them knowing of his whereabouts.

Wendy left the house one day to go over to her mother's house. Her sister and sister's boyfriend came to pick her up and when she got back home someone had broken into the house. They came in through the basement door, knocked the door half way off the hinges. They didn't damage the place but took some music equipment out of the basement. She did call the police.

She had a feeling something was wrong because the night before, when it was time to go to bed, she turned the lights off in the bedroom which is the back room, you can look out into the back yard where the basement is located. She heard noise like someone trying to break into the house. John was not home for some days and Wendy was mad. She got up and turned the light on in the bedroom and the noise stopped, after that, Wendy made sure her sister and her sister's friend didn't go anywhere until she checked the house.

John mentioned a place where he was going and she asked a friend of the family if they knew the area. He said, yes and took her over to the place where they found him. It took him a long time to come out; this was like a bad dream because she was lost and didn't understand. John didn't come home and Wendy moved everything out of the house. Her and her child's life were in danger, and she didn't waste any time getting out. That was all she needed, one negative threat, not knowing what this was all about, life or death.

Wendy called his father and mother, letting them know

something was going on and it was not good. She didn't want anything bad to happen to John. She moved back with her mom and John was in the street. Wendy did talk to him because it was their son's first birthday, he said he was coming up and he would be there. On the day, of their son's party everyone was waiting to sing happy birthday. No John, so they began singing happy birthday. The phone rang and it was the hospital. John was in a very bad car accident, it was a head-on collision. The other car came over the medium strip, and hit John head-on. He was hospitalized for a while. When he came out of the hospital, he went right back to his old ways for some time, but not too long.

John got a lawyer and after the settlement, they got another place and another brand new car. He was still dipping into some of his bad habits but not for long. This time he was back playing his music and in the house. John always wanted to make music but needed someone to sing to the beat. He even had rented out a few places and made it his studio. The men he was working with were just helping spend his settlement money.

The record deal never worked out. Wendy wanted him to buy her a used car but he didn't do it. He was getting high with those guys but you couldn't tell. As time went on, John came into the house and told her someone prayed for him. He was happy and went to church. Someone must have told John about the good news of Jesus Christ and how He died for our sins. Wendy never asked, how he got saved but John was going to church and serving the Lord. What a blessing. God can do anything but fail. He can take a person's mess and change it into a miracle. God can bless you in any circumstances and will meet you where you are at. He's not looking for perfect people, just lost souls, and a hurting person. If you just let God love you, let Him in your heart, He will take good care of you. The couple have two children now. In this relationship, Wendy didn't have to deal with cheating and being unfaithful. It was drugs and Christ. A turning point for John and Wendy. A happy moment for John. For Wendy some disappointment for her life.

What happened was once John got saved, he forgot about Wendy and the kids. He did try to explain a little to her but wasn't patient with her like she was with him. Wendy still didn't get it or wasn't hearing clearly about the word of God. She needed to take up some Bible classes, attend church too, to receive wisdom and knowledge of the word so she could understand the truth about her life.

John asked Wendy one time to go with him. His best friend asked her also, and she went. John didn't encourage her enough and show her God's agape kind of love. He talked about leaving her because they weren't married. But they already had the kids and all he had to do was ask her to marry him. But he wanted to change her but wasn't doing it the right way. He was leading her away from God and not toward God.

Wendy stayed home with the kids, cooked meals, kept the house clean, washed clothes and kept the kids neat. Everything that a wife should do, she did it. Only problem was she would drink beer every once in a while. She had cut down on drinking because she also knew he was serving God. She respected that but Wendy realized they were unequally yoked. Meaning she was pulling one way and he was going toward God. At this point, she was drinking sometimes and John was changing fast from drugs. That was great because it took some people a long time to quit and some never stop. Wendy didn't understand at first because she never left John and was there through thick and thin, the good and the bad, and the heartache and pain.

He just up and left them in the house alone and went to live with his parents. The children were little babies. Wendy loved him too, just another relationship where a person can walk out of your life at any given time. There are people that come in your life for a little while, a moment, for a season or for a lifetime. But God knows what is best for each and every one of us.

John told Wendy he was going to his mother's to stay because they weren't married. What a hurting feeling. Wendy said she wouldn't have had kids if she knew they weren't going to be together. You never know if the relationship would last anyway because the temptation is strong. But that is what the Bible teaches us and shows us how to live according to His word. We should have been married first, then had kids. He left her and the children with no phone service. Wendy had to use the phone one day, so her next door neighbor wasn't home so she asked the old lady across the alley from her to use her phone. The older lady asked, "Why did the children's father leave you without a phone and you might need a phone for the kids. She said, "That was a shame he left them like that". She used to take the children up to John's mother's house and drop them off with him. She was trying to get even and pay him back for her suffering. But Wendy was only hurting herself and the children. Wendy didn't want to experience that pain all over again like in her first relationship but the pain was back once again.

Wendy missed her kids because they had always been with her so she would go back and get them. Besides her little girl would just cry and cry until John would put her to sleep. Without them, she was feeling lonely. She started drinking trying to heal the hurt, pass the time away and try to find ways to get over him. She cried and cried, couldn't sleep, used to call him and ask why he was doing this to her and the kids? This was a hard relationship too because she had to raise the kids alone. They didn't cheat or disrespect each other, this was the word of God. So that hurt because most people break up because of lying, cheating, disrespectful, unfaithful, and sleeping around. This relationship was different, Wendy didn't know if she wanted to live but she had to think before she reacted. She had kids to live for and take care of, so she realized that her life was very important and God loved her too.

Wendy's turning point was deadly in this relationship. After he left she stayed single for a while in order to get over her crying, stress, hurt, pain, anger, bitterness, emptiness, unhappiness, negative thinking, and to stop trying to get even, and decide to go to church to see what they were talking about in church. So she asked her neighbor to go with her to Pastor Reid's church because she would listen to him on T.V. and they started going. It helped her to understand, much better but it still hurt deep down. Wendy told her-self if he didn't want her, she didn't want him. She needed to heal now and move forward.

Later Wendy started dating a nice man near her house. He had no children, had his own place, nice car and he always cleaned his car and his house stayed clean; he had a good paying job. All the men she picked had a job. They started talking and he accepted her children. One day they went out of town to Wendy's relative's house. Wendy did something dumb, she told the kids' father to come check on the place while she was gone. When they came back, the children's father came down a few days later and asked Wendy to marry him. She was happy but knew she was with someone else and that he was going to find out later.

John knew the neighbor Wendy was talking to but not

yet. She was trying to figure out how to break it off with the man. She was scared because he was a good man, treated her and the children nice. So she called him over one night while the kids were asleep and explained that she wasn't over the children's father. That she needed more time; he was mad and hurt. He had tears in his eyes and she did too. He said, "You sure this is what you want to do?"

Wendy said, "Yes!" She didn't end up with either one because she knew John was going to find out and he did.

Never get in any relationship just to try to heal your pain because it might not work. Stay single and give the body plenty of time to recover from what you have lost. What was missing in Wendy's life was Jesus Christ and Him alone. Nothing else but Jesus. He is the only one who can make you happy, our happiness is not in people, look to God. We fall because of a lack of God's knowledge. This relationship got Wendy's attention and was an eye opener. One thing she remembered, God brought her out of the first one and He will do the same for her again. As long as you have a little faith, small as a mustard seed and repent your sins, ask for forgiveness and pray to God. He will help you.

Wendy had plenty of growing up to do, maturing in Christ, and learning the Bible. Bible—Basic Instruction before Leaving the Earth. She thanked God for John's life and her life. Glad that God was able to lift John up out of the pit and help her find her way back to Jesus Christ, the hard way. They both are applying the word of God in their hearts. She forgave John and he forgave her. John bought a house and was spending time with the children. They both stayed single for about seven to eight years. Later they both got married to other people.

Before John got married he went to Wendy's house, told her to sit down because he had something to tell them. She told him she didn't need to sit down! John asked her and the children what would they think of him getting married. Wendy said that was fine with her and the kids were still small but said ok. Wendy had her man and he had his lady. Before they got married, he brought the lady to Wendy's house, to meet them all and Wendy's man was there too. They showed her around the house. She seemed like a nice person at that moment. The children were in John's wedding and went over to their father's house about three times since he was married. His wife did a u turn on Wendy's children.

John's wife started treating the children bad, didn't want Wendy's children around them or to spend family time with them after they got married. Wendy's children went to one family gathering at their father's house besides the wedding gathering. One day Wendy's daughter went over her dad's house and the wife was there but later left. They had one child at the time. John had stepped out for a minute but was coming back. After that Wendy's children were never invited back to their home again. John had five kids now by his wife and didn't bring the children around so they could get to know each other. His wife kept them from seeing Wendy's children. None of the children really knew each other and John wouldn't speak up. When John's mother and the family have something, his wife would come to the gathering for a few minutes. As soon as Wendy's children showed up, John's wife would take her kids and leave. They are all Christian and serve God. It is very important, not to look at people who go to church because some are looking for a wife, husband, boyfriend, girlfriend, some sleep with pastors and that is because they are not after God's own heart. They go to church for all the wrong reasons and not to learn the word of God or obey the Bible.

Wendy's daughter asked why her dad didn't spend much time with her! They couldn't understand how their dad preached a sermon sometimes at his church or someone else's church and treat them the way he did and didn't invite them. Wendy told them to just pray for their father and stay focused on Jesus Christ and that they don't have to act like him.

It took Wendy years to get over John but she took very good care of her children. If she never went through all these situations and trials, she wouldn't know that God could bring her out. She is a witness and have testimony of what God can do. This relationship had her seeking Christ and wanting to know more about Him. She is so glad God saved John and herself because she refused to see him go down like that on drugs and she wanted to stop drinking beer. She forgave him once she started growing in Christ Jesus and understood the word much better, her life was also better. They both were doing well, are friends and communicate with the children, even though the children don't see him much. She realized that God is amazing, awesome, a deliverer and healer. His love never fails, so try to forgive everyone. You are not alone. Amen.

Wendy's 3rd Story—
Her 1st Husband

AFTER THE SECOND RELATIONSHIP, Wendy had to ask God to hide her in His righteousness. He was her deliverer, healer and refuge. Wendy realized once she got connected to God, it is much easier to handle any circumstances that came her way. Instead of doing things her way and leading unto her own understanding. She had to examine herself and show herself approval, meaning (was she doing what the word of God says to do). She had to trust Him, believe His word, and know that His love never fails. Her faith grew as she matured in Christ-like-image (learning to forgive and love herself and others). <Dying> to self and putting on the whole armor of God. Wendy understood her life was not her own, she was alive in Christ and Christ in her. A change was on the way. People are always watching Christians to see what you do wrong and the devil is always busy. The devil set Wendy up again, years later with David. She fell for the trick and another relationship began.

Wendy's third relationship was worse than the other two. This relationship really helped her find her way back to Jesus Christ. It was the break through point in her life and never giving up on the Word of God. Wendy waited patiently on her husband after all they had been through over the years. It wasn't easy, all the heartaches, pain, hurt, disappointment, adultery, cheating, compulsive dishonesty and stress. Her husband had caused her to become bitter on the inside. There were times in her life when she wanted to give up, let go of all the pain, get rid of David, find someone else, cheat too, get even, do evil for evil and let him feel the pain she was feeling. It is much harder when one partner is trying to keep the relationship or marriage together and the other partner is not helping. Most women know what they want and how they would like to be treated by a gentlemen. Women also need to respect and show how much she appreciates her man, especially when he takes very good care of her and the family. Doing little things for one another daily can make a heart happy and a peaceful home. But know that God gave us real true love. Jesus Christ should be first in your life, not your wife, husband, children or family.

Before Wendy started talking to David, her mind, body and soul were trying to learn more about Jesus Christ. Her past relationships started out good and later hurtful as well.

Susan Sykes

The only difference was she never got married to the other men. Both past relationships lasted over five years or longer. For years she stayed single, focused on Jesus, worked and just took very good care of her two children. Meanwhile trying to get over a relationship or marriage without Christ in the midst just wasn't easy. Always allow space and give yourself plenty of time before jumping right back into another relationship. When you wait, your mind will be at peace and your heart will feel at ease. It takes time to get over someone you trusted with your heart and you truly admire. Wendy had to clear her mind, take as much time as needed to heal, and regain her strength.

Wendy met David at a job sight, where she was working in 1995. David wasn't working there but knew a few guys on the job. One morning, he asked her, "Can I buy you a cup of coffee"?

She answered, "No thank you because I never drink coffee". Pepsi was her cup of tea. He came on the job a few more times but they never dated. Wendy never saw him again until two years later. She had found a bus driving job making more money. David happened to get on her bus one day, he had just got off work. He sat in the back of the bus just staring at her. He was thinking, I want her. He had no idea that the woman driving the transit bus was the same one at the warehouse job. He started riding her bus more often when he got off work. Wendy always remembered his face but he had no clue she was the same woman he once was trying to get fresh with.

A couple of weeks went by and one day David decided to stay on the bus and ride to the end of the line. He started talking to Wendy and he rode back across town with her. He was trying to get to know her and this is how they started talking. They continued talking while he rode the bus with her that night. Questions were asked, like do you have someone? Do you have any children? Who do you live with? Many other questions were asked as well. He told her he only had two kids and was married before but no children in the marriage. He said he lived with his brother. The talking on the bus ride went on for a while between the two. David brought her a bracelet one night and said it was a little something from him. Sometimes Wendy would feel a shamed of him while he was on the bus talking to her sitting up front. People who sit in the back can see everything up front. His hair was nappy, the socks he wore revealed the heel portion was past his ankles and he needed some clothes. He was a nice person and seemed charming. Most relationships start out this way at the beginning. The person would always be kind and make you feel wanted.

The two began to date. David started to come over to Wendy's house. She cut his hair for him and they had a nice evenings together. Wendy had a boy and a girl. She cut her son's hair a lot. Later everything was going well, the two hit it off great and David moved in with Wendy. The two were intimate, the first time he came over. David said, "Wendy is the first woman who ever made love to me like that." They both worked, spent time with each other and he enjoyed her family. He lived in the projects, but Wendy was interested in a person's heart. The rest of the relationship and things for the future, they both could work out together. Out of the kindness of her heart, she brought David some clothes to wear so when they went out to a relative's house, he would have something nice to put on. He told Wendy someone stole all his clothes. She didn't believe that, he is a small man. He did mention a lot of people were always in the house where he lived. They would eat the food up, and drink up everything and people were still there when he got up to go to work. David said he didn't get much sleep and sometimes he had to walk all the way to work because he had no money.

That was a long walk across town. You spend your money for the house and others are there that don't work but eat up everything, that is disrespectful to the man of the house who is the only one working. You wake up in the morning with people lying around but you have to walk to work. Wendy listened to every word that came out of David's mouth.

Wendy went over to her mom's house for a cookout. David knew some of her family members. He had worked with her mother and the boy cousin. They remembered David and Wendy's family and he got along just fine. The family talked, laughed, and had a good time. David was all on the floor laughing, he enjoyed himself at the cookout. David had so many jobs, he wasn't lazy, always worked and if he lost a job, it wouldn't take long to find another one. Just remember this old saying, you never know a person until you live with them and a lot of times you still don't really know them. Life is a game to a lot of people. Even though everything seemed fine there was one thing Wendy noticed. When David's bills started going to the house for child support, she would take him downtown to check on the payment and he would be mad, claiming he had been paying his child support. He was going to child support a lot. Wendy asked to see the bills because he said they always took the money out of his check. She looked at the child support paper and counted the different numbers, it showed he had more than the two children. She showed him the paper, and told him it looked like he had more kids but David denied it and said, they made a mistake. Every time he went to child support he was in denial of having other kids and the number on the paper clearly showed the truth. Wendy left it alone because it would soon come to light.

It had been over a year now, things were being revealed, and information was coming out. One afternoon, David wanted to go visit one of his sisters. Wendy and David rode over to his sister's hair salon. He introduced Wendy to his sister and while they were sitting down, David's sister was talking to him. She told David that his children have been looking for him and that he needed to go see the kids. His sister told him he could still have his relationship but go see the kids. So she said she would call the children's mom to make sure it was ok for him to see the kids. David knew why he wanted to visit his sister. He knew they probably were looking for him but he must have been scared to visit the kids while he was with the other woman before Wendy. His sister stated that she would call him later on. The couple left, got into Wendy's car and she asked, "David do you have more children"?

He said, "I hope it's not going to interfere with our relationship". He had four children by his first wife, he said he didn't have any by her. That was a lie. The next day, David's sister called and gave him the number and address. The children had been looking for him for some years after he and their mom got a divorce.

David and Wendy received the information from the sister and went to see the children. Wendy met the children and their mom. They all were nice and very well mannered. David hadn't seen them in some years since he left their home. Wendy started dropping him off to spend time with the kids. Then go back and pick him up. Sometimes he wouldn't stay long, He would call Wendy and say he was ready. She would say you are ready to come home, you haven't been there long. Maybe David and the children didn't know what to talk about. The couple tried to stay in contact with the children and do little things with them. There was still a lot Wendy needed to know about David and his secrets. There were two more children she needed to meet and their mom. The other kids were by the lady he got stuck with, and after his wife found out he was cheating on her. David committed adultery, he had two children with his girlfriend and this is what caused the first marriage to end. They both had girls the same month and David gave both baby girls almost the same name. This lady weighed about 475 pounds, his girlfriend and David weigh about 120. He is a very small man. His first wife was tall but not heavy.

David always messed around on this lady too (his girlfriend). He had plenty of nasty books, that were hidden from Wendy but later she found the books. David was a compulsive liar. Wendy was the second wife. She always worked night shift and got off about 5 a.m. David explained to Wendy one day that he needed to go see his other children out of town because the daughter was sick. Wendy didn't know he had been talking to the ex-girlfriend with the other two kids while she was at work. He wasn't living with his brother either when Wendy started seeing him, that was a lie. He lived with the girlfriend who helped break up his first marriage but they moved out of town. The lie David was telling didn't sound right but Wendy let him go anyway. Who knows what he had been telling them while living with Wendy. He went and was down there sleeping with the children's mother, he did come back of course and told more lies. Do you see how a man that dog a woman and lie to them, how the lady gave them plenty of chances? They think that is love but it is not. You have some women who have been with their husbands from school to adulthood, for over 20 years and that man makes one mistake and the lady is ready to leave him. Or it can be the other way around, the woman made one mistake. David did plenty, so if your spouse did one thing in the marriage found God and try to work it out, take your vows seriously, to death do you part. It may seem hard but with God all things are possible. Wendy is a living testimony.

Months later, David wanted to go see the kids again. He made up something else and Wendy allowed him to go. That was Wendy, dumb to let him go again. This time David was talking about marrying her and the lady was in the background saying that they were going to get married. She knew he was talking to Wendy but every time she was able to get him in her presence, she controlled him. But he allowed her to control him. Yes, he wanted to see the children but she still had some kind of control over him. David had given her all his money. He had no more money to get back home. Maybe his kids did need him, Wendy didn't know what was going on. This lady had David beat up before for cheating on her. He was a nice man, cheater and also a weak man for women. David was so bold, he had got his wife and girlfriend pregnant at the same time. Both women had the children in the same month and a week apart. You can see why his first marriage didn't work out. Wendy only knew that he had all those kids, from looking at the child support papers and from what his sister said.

Wendy was so hurt, her and David were going to get married. She put her trust in her man, treated him good and was faithful. And this is what she got in return, a heart full of unhappiness, depression, stress, disappointments and plenty of lies. Wendy was so weak, she didn't want to go to work, she cried day and night. It was like another bad dream, with pain all over again and why did she fall again for the devil trick. There was no way David could get around out there where he went, he had no car and wasn't working down there. Wendy knew David was making the biggest mistake in his life. She found a phone number David had in the drawer, who was a relative to this girl, the children's mother. Wendy called the number and told the lady who she was to David, and the lady said he shouldn't have come down there and she should come and get her man. She said she didn't know why he came down because they are still doing the same old stuff. That is how, Wendy got the address. David's best friend and Wendy went to pick him up and David's 475 pound girlfriend came to the door with a sheet wrapped around her.

David's best friend went to the door and David came out. He talked to David and told him Wendy was with him and that she was in the car. The men walked to the car and they all had a nice talk. He didn't want to leave the kids and who knows if he really wanted the kid's mom. But as long as he was with someone else, she wouldn't let David see the children. He went back in the house to get his things and they left. David had a very bad odor, it was like he didn't have a bath in days. Wendy had to be a good woman and a crazy woman to go get him. The things people do when they think they are in love. She must have really loved him or wanted to continue to help him. David said he would stay with one of his sisters if Wendy didn't want him to come back to her. But she took him back in and his mother told Wendy, you never send your man away to another woman or to see the kids alone. She should have gone with David. David went down there twice and that is because he probably was talking to the kids too and they wanted to see him. Being sneaky while Wendy was at work and thinking, how can I explain to Wendy? That was a mess and now the trust is broken. David never went down there again.

The couple were back working again and they were working on the relationship as well. But there is a big problem, Wendy can't forget the lonely nights, how she cried day and night, missed time from work, being bitter, angry, couldn't eat, and was drinking. She tried to trust him but about three years later, the ex-girlfriend moved back near David and Wendy. Once David found out he went around there twice before he told Wendy. He probably never got rid of the lady's number and was still talking to her and the kids. Maybe

David was trying to see the kids and make their mom think he wasn't with anyone. When David told Wendy he wanted her to go over there with him, she went with him. But David wasn't the one who told Wendy that he had already been over there a few times, one of the neighbors told her. David knocked on the door and asked to see the kids, the kid's mom asked who Wendy was. David said, "His wife", and the lady would not let him see the kids, his daughter came out but the mother made her go back in.

A couple of days later they were calling David and the mother told him to come but not to bring his wife. He explained that Wendy was coming. He knew his tail was already in hot water. Wendy was going to sit in the car while he talked to the children, since their mom wouldn't let him bring them to their house. This situation was a mess. This was a Daddy's children, Mama drama. David and his wife had to go to the courthouse in order for him to see his kids. David went alone and the kids showed up one time and never again.

A month later she moved the kids out of the state again so David couldn't see them because he was with Wendy, his second wife. David refused to fall for her tricks and lose what he had again. By breaking up David's first marriage, she also lost him.

David was still seeing the children from his first marriage. One day the kids came over the house and were having a good time. That was too much noise for David but Wendy loved kids so the noise didn't bother her. The couple were all the way upstairs in their bedroom. David came downstairs and was arguing with them and one of the daughters didn't like what he said. A few minutes later, his daughter came upstairs and said something about the way he talked to them. They got into a big argument. He called his daughter out her name and all of the kids were mad. Wendy was nice enough to take them home. She didn't want to take them home like that and explain to their mom what happened. It was not good. The next day David and Wendy went over to the children's house to explain the incident to their mother. He said the daughter should never come to his house again but the other ones could. The mom told him he shouldn't have called her what he did. After that, he didn't see them for some years. How can you tell one of your kids to never come over again? Of course the other ones are not going to come either. Now they are upset with David. For some reason David doesn't seem like a father role model. A few years later, the kids tried to get in touch with David. He started seeing them again for some years but now his wife Wendy was mad at him because he couldn't be trusted as usual. He was still lying and playing games.

David started his cheating and lying. He said, he would be going one place and be somewhere else. He started to hide his phone, his wallet and pay stubs. He didn't want to show Wendy his pay stubs with nothing on them because child support always took his money. He had more than five children. The trust had already been broken a long time ago but she was trying to forgive him and trust him again. David would be talking on the phone to ladies and when his wife would come in the room, the phone flew out his hand and across the room. So you knew he was doing something wrong to throw the phone.

One time David acted like he was going to drive for a bus company. A trip out of town for about three to four days. The story again didn't make sense, he was up to no good. Wendy said you could tell he was hesitant about going because he knew he was wrong and they were married. She was still a little mad anyway and didn't care. David went on the trip, it was cold outside, snow on the ground and when he got to where ever he went, he didn't call his wife at all. He was gone for four days. Who knows what he did for years while she was on night shift. She did pick up on a few but he had done some stuff.

Wendy was hurt, worried, depressed and angry. She couldn't wait until he got home. She also had to shovel the snow and there was a lot. Wendy was pissed. When he got in, he told her there was no service at all. She told him, you could have used somebody's phone or called collect. But that was ok because Wendy already had called out from work. What was done, was done and there was nothing she could do about it but take care of business now.

Once he mentioned that he stayed in his room and didn't go out. That he only went out to find something to eat and that these big women were walking around in their swim suits and they said something to him. He pretended he didn't do or say anything back and the whole time those were the same ladies he went away with because Wendy talked to one on the phone. He always acted like he didn't like big women, but would always mention something negative about their size. He just tried to throw a person off so you would think he didn't like them. When Wendy first met him, he was with a big woman. David loved big women, he only weighed about 120 pounds. Every time he got caught cheating, that is who he would go to for love and end up with. There is nothing wrong with big boned women but no one wants a man like that playing with their feelings. He tried to find the bigger women who didn't drive. Someone who he thought he could put something over on, but some of them didn't take no mess off from him either. He loved smiling in your face and stabbing you in the back. Wendy pretended she was going to work. She got in the car he drove, which was hers. It was a mess in the car. All the music, CDs, another phone and women's belongings were thrown in the back under the trunk of the car. He had sex or a party going on in that car. Satan really had him. She went back in the house and they went at it.

He didn't drive that car for a while. Things really started getting worse in the marriage. David had to walk or ride a bike when he went out. The marriage was a mess. Wendy wanted to knock his head off his shoulders but little as he was she might have killed him. Wendy knew he wasn't worth going to jail for. There are always other ways around the pain and most of the time it is best to talk or walk away. Calm down and get yourself together because you can't do anything when you are mad but only regret it later. Love is really blind sometimes. Try not to bring curses to your children because of what has happened to you. If you are a true believer in Christ, do right by the Bible because Jesus sees everything we do, the bad and good. But we should be loving and caring at all times and to everyone. It takes real change in the heart and mind.

Wendy became bitter and was going to get even. She stopped talking to him because she knew mostly everything that came out his mouth was a lie. If he tried to talk to her, she would ignore him. But she realized that her attitude wasn't of God's nature. She would respond to some things but made sure it was brief. Wendy would go over to a friend's house and stay until morning. So, he could see just how it felt, not knowing where your other half was and if they were sleeping around. David always used the fire station to escape and for an excuse, he volunteered there and loved staying overnight. Sometimes he wasn't there. Wendy started putting the tail out of the house and that is where David would go, to the fire station or somewhere else. She had stopped drinking beer but things got bad so she started back up. Even though David was wrong, Wendy took him back and maybe that is why he kept being disrespectful. Because he was getting away with the lies. Women and men sometimes love the other person but they don't really love you. We have to let them go and move on especially if you are not married. Stop crying, move on because God might have something better for you. Why worry about a person who makes your life miserable. Sometimes we as ladies need to also check ourselves and see where we are falling short in the marriage. There is always two sides to a story. Wendy put him out a few times and she was getting tired of it. The same old stuff, going around and around in a circle, and getting the same result.

This marriage was in trouble and it was sad. This is a marriage you don't want to remember. It is only what you allow a person to do and get away with which causes them to continue doing wrong. David did start the cheating and Wendy had been through enough and couldn't believe marriage was this miserable.

David was able to see his kids by his first wife again after a few years of their argument. Anyway, by him hurting Wendy so bad, she started not to care too much about anything. The kids and their mom weren't the only people he hurt. He did lots of bad things in his second marriage with Wendy. The kids had no idea, it wasn't that Wendy was mean to their dad but he was very disrespectful. They did know that sometimes Wendy put their dad out because one of his daughter's boyfriends help him move his things out of the house. Their dad was doing the same thing he did in his first[t] marriage (cheating and sleeping around). Wendy had enough from her past relationships and she wasn't going to let him get away with hurting her. She kept taking him back but he continued to still be sneaky. Lastly, Wendy separated from him for about one year and six months. She did see him a few times on the street and talked to him a few times. He still was sleeping around and searching for love in all the wrong places. His wife continued, to observe him in his pride and sinful nature. David continued to test the waters and he did just what the devil knew he would do. Is it really worth your marriage and home? Most persons do bad things to get even with their mate because they don't know how to fix their relationship. It takes communication and love from both persons. We all just want to be love and for the spouse to show that they care. Most of the people in bad marriages get a divorce because they don't know how to fix the problem. The marriage isn't broken they just don't take time out to get to the root of the problem and fix it. The couple can't do it alone but with Jesus Christ all things are possible. Jesus is the answer to all pain, hurt, disappointments and bad situations.

What happened the last time was a woman called on his wife's phone and left a message. It said, I am home now and you can come over. Oh, Wendy was mad because they were trying to still work on the marriage, however, things seem to be falling over the hill. Satan always attacked her husband in order to get to Wendy and it worked. How did the lady get Wendy's cell phone number? Or was this other lady being smart? Wendy was upset again, she packed David's clothes and took him up to his mom's house. He stayed at his mom's and he later found some lady to live with. Another heavy set lady, who he talked about in order to try to throw his wife off. However, these are the kind of women he really enjoyed. Again, women are women and we all have feelings, so be careful who's feelings you mess with. He even went to church with her. Knowing he was sinning, married, but listening to the word while the Holy Spirit convicted him. The word of God was going in one ear and out the other ear. He was a man who can't obey, the message that the Pastor taught because of his sinful nature. But he wasn't alone and many people are like this. Wendy used to be that way before too. David didn't care, he was raised in the Word of God. A lot of people hate to change and they enjoy their sinful nature. Some people like feeling good for a moment. He used to tell the lady he loved her and she told him the same thing. Love doesn't hurt but tells the truth, certainly not David.

David went to church but always came out worse off and had no fruit to show. He was a devil behind a mask. He acted one way in church and another way outside of church. People forget, God can see everything. David heard the Word but was not a doer of the Word. He never wanted to pray with his wife because of the demons inside of him. His love was waxed cold and he couldn't handle the word of God, the trials in his life or going to the cross, asking for true forgiveness. He always slipped backward and was around negative people and he ran from his first love who is Jesus. He needed his mind to be transformed into a Christ-like-image and that is why Wendy, tried to hang in there and do the will of our Lord and Savior Jesus Christ. A woman after God's own heart, wanting to share God's love and patience. She wanted David to know that God still loved him and she did too. Wendy did her part because she had faith and trusted God and His word. His word has power.

In David and Wendy's marriage, she took marriage vows very serious. This was her first marriage and wished no bad luck on any relationship or marriage. Wendy had never expected something like this to happen in her marriage. Marriage is what God requires between male and female. It shouldn't be miserable like this but sometimes it is. Thank God for the Holy Spirit, that revealed many things for Wendy to see. Just like the lady called, her phone for her husband, the evidence found in the car, staying away for days and pretending he had no service, he use to go places and he would hit his phone by a mistake and Wendy would hear everything. Through all of these different situations nevertheless this woman had to be strong and stay focused on Jesus Christ.

Now they are separated and Wendy had to draw back to God. The one who is able to keep us from falling. She had put in for two divorces but David didn't want that. Wendy continued do what the Lord commanded. She tried to forget about her husband but she was a little worried about him and hoping he was ok. This was the longest they had ever been apart from each other. David was hurt but refused to do what was right and Wendy needed her Lord and Savior to heal the pain and sorrow. We fall down but Jesus can help us get back up again.

The Second Half of Pride in David

It has been over a year now, since the separation. Some men and women don't like to admit when they are wrong and don't like to apologize. Wendy stayed focused on Jesus, He's first priority in her life. She is covered by the blood of Jesus Christ and nothing can separate her from His love. Next, she continued being faithful to the Word of God. She didn't have to sleep around just because David was still doing his own thing. Her body was the temple of the Holy Spirit and she belonged to Christ now. Her mind was on work and taking care of the children. She prayed for her husband and left him in God's unchanging hands. Also for herself, she prayed for God to work on her and show her, His plan for her life. Wendy talked to his mother every so often and still went to see her. David's mom always came over to the house to help them both to understand the Bible and how to live as a family. The mother would talk to both of them about husband and wife and the role of a husband and wife. It would work sometimes for a minute but not long. When the trust is broken, it can be so hard to get the relationship back right and most of the time it never gets right. What a hurting feeling.

Sometimes at night Wendy might would want to call her husband but she didn't want to go through more disappointment. One day she was talking to her mother in law and she said David wanted to know if he could have her phone number. She changed the number so he wouldn't call her while she was trying to get over him. Or so she wouldn't be looking at her phone saying, he hasn't called so he must not love me or care. Many people, men and women do that, when they break up with someone they truly care about. His mother would always tell him that he needs to go home to his wife because she didn't raise David like that. When you truly love someone, love just don't disappear like that. You want it to work on the marriage but you hate the pain it caused. We can't change a soul or make them want us, only God can change a person. Wendy had to accept things as they were, ask God for direction and understanding. She gave David's mom permission to give David the phone number.

They separated in the middle of 2010 and started back talking close to the end of 2011. Wendy did run into him a couple of times on the street, out of the blue. Anyway the couple started talking again and David asked Wendy if she loved him. She said, yes and she asked him the same question before. His answer was, yes but not in love with you. They both might not love each other anymore, or they are confused. By both of them hurting each other, it has really caused some damage in each other's lives. If two people are together, one pulling this way and the other another way, the relationship isn't going to work. They are unequally yoked. The best relationship is when both persons are after God's own heart. David was the opposite and won't listen to his calling in life.

They start seeing each other again and he wasn't working for a while. So, she got him a job where she was working. He had left the lady's house who he was staying with, so he could get his own place. Maybe the Word of God touch his heart and the things his mom told him. Most of the time people do things because they are hurting. They use other person's thinking that will help them get over the one they love. Trying to heal what was broken but the problem is still there because they didn't allow themselves to breathe and heal the pain. We want peace but also want the one we love. David had his place now. He was on his way over his wife house when the car broke down. The job came through, he had no more car and the job is right down the street from Wendy's house. He ended up staying with her the whole week and she would take him home on Friday. Sometimes she made him catch the bus. She would go over his house every once in a while and leave. Wendy could feel something wasn't right.

This man had so many chances to get his marriage

right, however that sinful nature the devil wouldn't let him go. David wasn't strong enough to fight the devil back. But David allowed Satan to have control over him. Once David started working with Wendy, he became friends with a man there. This man, named Peter got David going to his church and David was doing great. The Pastor even prophesized over David and told him, "If you go back to doing what you were doing you will die." He became a Deacon at the church and was faithfully going to everything the church had. But something was wrong with the picture. David was talking to the lady, he was living with but was lying to her. David was sleeping with her every once in a while, and was staying at his wife's house to go to work. The wife knew something wasn't right. That is why she won't stay or go to his house. He was going to church and he needed to get rid of the sin in his life. David and Wendy had straightened up his place one day and he said, that means you want a key to the house. Wendy told him no because she wasn't going to be coming over there and she didn't. She was fed up with that foolishness and David needed to grow up. He had a chance to be strong and stop sinning while living alone. That is why, Wendy stayed away because David needed to be strong and mature. He needed Jesus badly but just wouldn't let God in, the devil had a very strong hold on him. David can't seem to break the chains off of himself because he needed God's help. David always run from God, never to Him.

The man on the job, Mr. Peter, started a prayer circle. David, Wendy, First lady from another church and a few others from the job would attend. When praying on one subject David was the only one who would pray something different. Especially if it had something to do with relationships. David was acting weird, Wendy knew when he was doing wrong. She walked in her bedroom one night, David hung up the phone but that was fine, same old ways.

One day, David was off to church, Wendy went to a different church, the church she attended for years and David hopped from church to church. When he left, for church one of his phones was laying on the desk, so Wendy looked through the phone and called one of the numbers. Only because of David's actions. She called the number and a woman answered. Wendy asked, "What is your relationship to David?"

The woman was trying to get smart. She said, "Ask him who I am!

Wendy told her, "I'm his wife and the way you act is why the men do what they do." Wendy explained, how she doesn't like men playing around with women's feelings. Both women start talking for hours and Wendy got all the information she needed from the lady. She told her everything about her and David. She said, they had stopped talking. They were talking as friends but they were texting that they loved each other.

Wendy asked for the lady's address and went over her house that night. David kept calling Wendy because he also knew when she had found out something. And that's not good! The women sat outside in Wendy's car and talked for hours; they were already talking for hours when Wendy was at home. She showed Wendy the text message and said they both had naked pictures of each other. She said, David also had a pair of her underwear. Wendy got home and told David, she met the lady, that the lady told her mostly everything and what was going to happen in the marriage, from this day forward.

Even though they were apart from each other, David should have been at least trying to have a better relationship with all his children. No, he was still chasing women. The same thing he did in his first marriage. This lady had given him a book," Why Men Love Bitches?" What an example for David's daughters, if they came to his place. Wendy asked, him why was he reading something like that. He lied and said a lady at Skateland let him read it, so the devil still had that body.

When Wendy got to work that Monday she let the prayer group know what was going on. Peter was surprised because his whole church loved David and gave him a title and knew nothing about him. Mr. Peter asked, Wendy if her and David were really married. The people at his church always asked, that question and Peter would tell them, he didn't know.

Wendy didn't want to go to prayer at work, if David was going. She didn't have time for him to keep smiling in her face and stabbing her in the back, and putting a front on for others. The marriage needed help. Wendy wanted David to leave but he wanted them to go to counseling with his Pastor.

David set up an appointment with the Pastor. They both went and the Pastor listened to both sides of their stories. Pastor told David it was his fault for all that happened, that he needed to change his number, start dating his wife again and that he had to build the trust etc. The Pastor also told David he needed to move back in with his wife but she really didn't want that right away. David on the other hand, wanted that and he broke his lease and would not go back to that place at all. He knew that once he went home, Wendy wasn't going to let him come back to her house. Because she was going to think about what he was still doing. When he did go back to his place, they both were moving his stuff out and into storage. It went well for a while. David is a little better but have left God's side again. It could be because his children didn't want anything to do with him. David is no longer in church and his wife decided that he needed to make his own decision because he knew right from wrong, we all do. He goes to work and comes home. He does go bowling with a friend, who is a pastor but he stayed in the house most of the time with his wife. God is faithful and is good. Wendy is attending Bible College and staying focused on Christ.

There are plenty more marriages, that are worse off than Wendy and David's. But their marriage helped show that no relationship is a piece of pie but takes a lot of work. Stay tuned for my next book to see how this marriage is going, it is now 2017 and we are still hanging in there so far. When a person loves someone, they will try to make it work. People have to communicate, have trust and show love. Without trust and communication, there is no relationship. Christ has to be the first priority in each person's life; have a relationship with Jesus, and the one you trust and depend on when heavy storms arrive. Not your relatives or anyone else. Your best answers and who to follow is Christ. Christ is the center of everything in your life. It doesn't matter what they have done, just forgive everyone so you can be free from all the pain that people may have caused you. It really does hurt when you trust someone and they betray you. You gave your heart, body, attention and all of your love, to get disrespected for no reason. The marriage can work but are you willing to try? It takes two, just like it takes two people to have a child and two people to get married. Once married, you both become one. Love Jesus, love yourself, neighbors, then you will be able to love others.

How Wendy Overcame
Hatred for her Husband

BY A GENTLE HEART Wendy overcame hatred, bitterness and pain. Wendy Black recognized, once again her heart was broken and God brought her out of other relationships in the past and He can help her again. There was something missing in her life, it was her Lord and Savior Jesus Christ. She had to remember, Christ died on the cross for our sins and he shed his blood for our sins. So that we may live, be set free and have an abundant life. The mind has to be fixed on Jesus Christ, wanting more of Him and less of yourself. She had to have a hunger and thirst after, Jesus Christ's heart and wanting to be more like Him. Wendy stepped back, let go of the situation and let God handle it. We don't have to fight our battles alone because God is there by our side. He will never leave us nor forsake any of us. It was a divine purpose for her life, once she let God in and she called on Him for help.

Wendy refused to continue on being carnal minded,

double-minded and unstable in all her ways. There had to be a change in her thinking, her mind and a change of heart. She wanted a heart full of God's agape kind of love, tender hearted, kind and peaceful. Something that can rub off of her onto other people, who's heart was crushed and empty. God has called us to trust Him, have faith, believe in Him, study the Word of God and have a heart willing to serve others. She wanted a heart that can show love, give love, speak love, and people would appreciate it. A merry heart that is willing to win broken hearts for the Savior. Keeping a spiritual heart, a personal relationship with Christ, read the Bible, heart full of love, equipped with God's knowledge, be a true believer and doing the work of God. These things helped her overcome hatred in the mind and heart. Wendy had to have her heart healed before she was able to help anyone else. God makes all the difference in people's lives, by the washing of His Word. God sees our hearts and knows us inside and out. Be thankful that somebody is praying for us all. We all need it.

This lady knew that God wanted to bless her but she had to exchange her bitter heart, for God's agape love which is unconditional. This kind of love makes a heart full of joy. Wendy surrendered all of her heart, mind, body and soul to Him. A heart full of sadness, is no good for your health, nor peace of mind, nor joy; being evil, doing evil for evil, getting revenge on a person and holding on to an unforgiving spirit is bad. Wendy had to get rid of the negative mind-set. A

Susan Sykes

miserable heart, keeps a person in bondage, in a box, gives place to the devil because you have an open door for demons to enter in. Wendy changed all of that into patience, just waiting on the Lord.

They that wait on the lord should renew their strength and He shall strengthen your heart. (Psalm 27:14).

God was able to use her where she was at, in time of trouble. He met her with that broken heart and turned things around for her good. She now has a healthy heart which is spirit filled. Maturing every day, growing in Christ character and nature. She has moved out of Satan's worldly kingdom into God's kingdom of righteousness. Wendy's heart is getting better day by day, with the meditating of God's Word. (The Bible). God can do anything but fail. Give that unforgiving spirit to Him then He will give you a new heart.

Forgive overcome hatred

When Wendy forgave the men, in each of her relationships and marriage, it made a big difference in her life. She was slowly able to move on but she was taking small steps. Gradually she made it to the healing process. She began smiling again, came out of her dark closet, her strength came back, her desire to do things was back and she always enjoyed helping others. We sometimes can give encouraging words to others but we won't follow them ourselves when we are down and hurting.

Forgiving can be one of the hardest, things to do but that is why Wendy had to call on Jesus Christ. She got tired of going to church but never coming into the true knowledge and experience of Christ or the Holy Spirit. If she, continued holding on to hatred, the pain would still be inside her and won't go away that easy. There is joy, peace, victory and power in the name of Jesus, when we go to him in prayer. Wendy had to go to Jesus Christ in prayer, ask him to search her heart, and see if there was any wicked ways or bad attitude in her. And if it was to cleanse her, renew the right spirit in her and make her whole, into His image. To learn more of Him and his ways. You should always repent your sins and ask God to forgive you.

Forgive and get rid of the strongholds in your life. An unforgiving spirit can weigh you down, make you very weak, unable to think but with our Lord and Savior, we can get back up again. Amen. What a miserable feeling to have when we are unforgiving. It shows that our souls are wounded and need to be loved by God. Be careful of Satan's devices, treats, and snares. Satan enjoys keeping confusion going in your family, on the job, in relationship, marriage, and people's homes. When we forgive, it can take care of lots of problems, so don't allow Satan to steal your joy and happy home. Remember God forgave us, so we should forgive everyone, as well, you are not alone. People aren't going to treat you the way you want them to but they are only human, and none are perfect. Move forward and don't look back into your past, unless it's a testimony for you. After knowing Christ, then you want to be filled with the Holy Spirit, to lead, direct, guide you and teach you all things to come. Knowing that God is a good God, He's a great God and He can do anything but fail, this should help you love and forgive one another. It's about Wendy's attitude and reaction to a situation which made her the person she is today, successful and able to forgive.

(Roman 12:21) be not overcome by evil, but overcome evil with good. 21 Century King James Bible.

Our hearts, minds, attitude, reactions, and the way we think is something we deal with every day of our life. They show a person's real attitude and their true personality. Be positive in each one, demonstrating God's love toward others daily. All these things can help build a person up in love, strengthen your mind, deal with your emotions better and help you have a change of heart. Forgive and have victory, have a river of water flowing through and inside of you. Be thankful for each day, thank your parents because you wouldn't be here today and thank the Creator of the world, whose name is Jesus Christ. Forgive people and do it in the name of Jesus. Move forward and don't look back because the past sometimes can be painful but things do happen for a reason. Some things in our life are only there for a little while and not forever. It is so important that you, stay focused on Jesus Christ. He is our redeemer, savior, helper, peacemaker and there is no one like Him. The Bible teaches us to forgive, just as God forgave us. Amen. (Luke 6:37) Judge not, and ye shall not be judged. Condemn not, and ye shall not be condemned. Forgive and ye shall be forgiven. 21 Century King James Bible.

Face your fears head on and stop running away from people who have hurt you and stop refusing to listen to God. God says, to forgive and make peace with all men. It is a testimony when you can forgive and your life would be full of peace. Avoid letting the unforgiving spirit, take over your life and control you. Wendy had to speak to the devil out loud and put him in his place. He has no place in her life anymore, enough is enough.

Wendy was relaxed, her brain could think and forgiving made way for her new life. It helped her with her high blood pressure, stress, hostility, depression, heart aches, and allowed her to have a better understanding and improve her immune system. When she forgave it also helped her see the truth about herself, overlook the childish for she knew not what she was doing. Some people do what they shouldn't do and don't do what is right. When we do things outside of the will of God, it separates us from Him and we appear to be different from God's knowledge of truth. We have not known the mind of Jesus Christ and His voice. She believes that forgiving is one of the most important lessons that human being are here to learn and it's healthy for the mind and body. This is the spiritual aspect of forgiving and overcoming bad memories, in our life.

Unforgiving spirit- Being Set Free

Wendy used to cry in the dark, couldn't sleep, was bitter because of all the pain. An unforgiving heart will stop or keep you from living the life God has intended for you. That life is abundant life, love, joy and full of Jesus Christ Himself. A person's heart grows cold, they become ill, miserable, and empty on the inside. They begin to act their shoe sizes and immaturely because they have been hurt by someone they loved. Many don't know how to fix the problem, they know what the Bible says but refuse to do so. Try not to be rude, disrespectful, continue to suffer and be tormented by the devil. An unforgiving spirit wants revenge, holds grudges for years, becomes violent, is hateful, mean, and their behavior gets worse. They can't think right, they have mental and emotional breakdowns and they teach their children to not forgive. When people are unforgiving, stress, and worry can bring sickness and disease upon yourself. Be stress free by forgiving and loving, be kind to each other because love never fails.

An unforgiving spirit is not worth becoming unhealthy, weak, and hiding behind a mask or clown face. Let the attitude of forgiving replace the unforgiving spirit with the beauty of God's love shining like the bright sun. You want people to see your light because what is hiding on the inside of you that people don't see will eventually come out of you and everyone will see your true character and nature. Avoid thinking about things that have already been done and spend time talking to God, on how to forgive. Stop living in denial, anger, confusion and frustration, it's not worth the pain. Break free from imprisonment and blaming others for your hurt and pain; all have made mistakes. An unforgiving spirit is a sin and it stands in between a person and God's real true love. We all are sinners and everyone needs a great forgiveness of love. We all deserve hell but thanks to God, so just look at yourself in the mirror and things you have done or said to someone. Did God forgive you? You can't love someone, if you have something against anyone/person. We all have our ups and downs but God is able to turn things around and help us to forgive.

Go beyond hate and forgive. If you want everlasting joy learn to love, forgive, and when things don't turn out the way we want, still show love. Life is challenging and isn't always fair but our Heavenly Father knows what is best for us. He understands, what we are going through but we have to still keep His commends and obey His word. Refuse to continue hurting others, do no evil, no pay back, but know that forgiving is the right thing to do in God's eyes and not doing things your way. Life is too short to live miserable, the next day is not promised to anyone and time doesn't wait for anyone. Forgive, love, be kind, gentle and have a heart after God's own heart. Putting God first, His agape love and forgiving can heal, deliver also set a person free from unforgiving attitudes.

Susan Sykes

Listen to the Small Voice

Wendy, as she began to understand what was happening in her life all these years, realized she was missing God's small voice. We have to be aware of the voices that speak to us. Whose voice is it? Is it God or someone else? Listening to other voice and people can get you in plenty of trouble. Be aware of your surroundings and the people you get involved with because everyone is not a true friend to the end. When things keep happening in your life and you can't understand why. Most of the time God is trying to get our attention and we don't realize it because some of us doesn't have an intimate relationship with God. God is calling all of us, to the cross, so we can live righteous in Him. (Luke 6:27) "But, I say unto you that hear; love your enemies, do good to them that hate you. 21 Century King James Bible. When you learn to listen, be patient, respect and obey God word than you will have a chance to be happy. Live life in love, by comforting hurting people as well as other person who need the love of God in their life. Listening to God will help discipline yourself, forgive, apologize, be honest and practice love. Are you tired of living the same way? If so, seek first the Kingdom of God and everything else will be added unto you. Get a fresh start in life, pray and when you hear the small voice of God, you will experience the fruit of the spirit. These are the fruits of the spirit, agape love, faith, goodness, joy, peace and kindness. Are you bearing good fruit?

Wendy truly needed a Savior based on the fact that she knew God loved her and that was the kind of love needed at the time in her relationships and marriage. Her mind needed to be renewed at this point in time. She went back to church, praising, worshipping, singing, dancing and giving thanks to our Lord. Fellowshipping with other's beliefs, as a matter of fact, can help build a person up in love. It did help Wendy. Once you draw back to God, concerning the matter of the mind, your attitude begins to change. The mind begins to think positive and starts moving toward your goal in life, while leaving the past behind. Her thinking began to change to that of a child of the Most High. As you go through life, you will always need God's support, to heal and deliver you from bad mind-sets. When we think in the flesh, your mind will have us thinking all kind of bad behavior. Having a forgiving mind helps you think better, renew the right spirit in you, help to believe, have faith, refresh the mind, and be loving toward everyone. It shows the living evidence of Christ in a person and how they came to a realization.

Wendy Black had to think the best for people, have a mind full of peace and a Christ-like mind. Having a spiritual righteous walk (meaning walking up right) in Jesus. She understood a righteous walk can keep the mind free from Satan's negative devices. Wendy was able to think much better, by taking into consideration she was able to control her thinking. The mind is a terrible thing to waste and destroy. God is there to meet our every need. What He starts, He will finish in your daily living. What a better way of walking instead of in the flesh. Where the mind goes, it places a major emphasis on the brain. Your mind can wander off, as a person thinks negative, therefore it makes the body follow the thinking pattern. Be respectful no matter what, follow the righteous ways of God while enjoying Him forever. This is another way Wendy escaped the stress, disappointment, shame, mistreatment and adultery in her marriage. Jesus is the way, truth, light and life.

Wendy's mind was set on the things from above in the midst of the problems she experienced. She asked, God to create a clean heart, in her and renew the right spirit within her. (Psalm 51:10). 21 Century King James Bible. All good gifts come from heaven and not from the world. A mind can be dangerous or understanding. Obey the commands in the Bible, change your mind, convert back to Jesus and you will be able to lean on Him. Trouble comes when we take matters into our own hands. The Bible teaches us to lead not into our own understanding but be delivered (Proverb 3:5). When you have the mind of Christ, we learn how to handle our situations in a different way, as well as think a different way. The mind would be a little more at peace. Wendy refused to let anyone destroy her mind again, under any circumstances in which she has no control over but pray for change in herself, through the knowledge of wisdom and the Holy Spirit.

Letting God Love You

There will come a time in your life when you just don't know which way to turn, where to run or who to run to. When you have done all you can but can't figure out where you went wrong, pray and be still. Dealing with an unstable marriage or relationship Wendy had to let God love her. All the cooking, cleaning, ironing clothes, nice home, peace in the home, quiet, gave your heart and the love, it makes you feel small. What do people want in a marriage? Or they just don't have any remorse for anyone's feeling. Many people are damaged because others have let them down, in one shape of form or another. Others are not used to a person treating them nice. Wendy realized only God could give her everything she needed. She made a decision and began to, just let God love her as she continued to love Him back. Just letting God love you, is very important and heals many souls. Letting God love you, when you don't deserve it requires a need and teaches us how to become a better problem solver.

Wendy thanked God for His love that does not hurt but heals. Letting God love you is a way for peace, fasting, prayer consideration, we learn to be patient with our husbands and wives. Teaches us how to love Jesus, ourselves, neighbors, and others. Never give up on a loved one, let go of the pride and take responsibility for all wrong reaction. Her husband, never admitted he was wrong and didn't say he was sorry.

David knew he didn't deserve Wendy at all in light of the fact that if only David could have stayed focused on Christ and let Him love him David might be a much better person, to a certain degree, surrendering to and keeping God's invitation of Salvation. He needed God to wash him clean. (Psalm 51:2) wash me thoroughly from mine iniquity, and cleanse me from my sin. 21 Century KJ Bible. Just letting God love him, would have helped with the marriage and how to take care of a family. What God put together, let no one come in between, especially in this day and age. Watch out for the devil's tricks and snares. You are not alone and Satan is busy.

Wendy had to use tough love on David and love him from a distance. Sometimes you do have to leave your loved one, in order for them to realize what they had. Maybe than they would know how to treat you the next time and if not you, maybe the next woman or man that comes their way. Be stable, not unstable or a double minded person.

Finance was a big problem in their marriage. David like blowing money and wasn't worried about the future. Never sat down with his wife to talk about buying a home, how to pay of bills, and learn to save. She mainly had everything or make decisions while David said nothing. She wished, he wasn't so hooked on material things but he was. He really needs God to come into his heart and love him. David might think, God won't forgive him for all the wrong he had done. David knows what the Bible says about Jesus, He forgives all who come to

Him and repent. The Lord is waiting with His arms opened wide, to just love anyone who draw near to Him. David just wouldn't change. (Psalm 55:19) because they do not change, therefore they do not fear God. 21 Century KJ Bible.

Don't look to anyone in this world to give you happiness, your happiness comes from God alone. You measure it by your call. Some people refuse to leave the old sins of nature and take up their cross. David was the same way, he would put self- first and become a lover of himself. We are here to fight a good fight. Let God in and He will love you and lead us on the right path of righteousness. He can show us what both persons are to do in marriage, head of household, with the children, finance-money, and as a married couple. Spending time with each other is so important because life is very short and the next day is not promised to anyone. We came in this world alone and are leaving with nothing. Cherish one another while you can and tell them how much you love them daily.

The average person doesn't know God, only about Him. People deny God's power but He can do anything but fail. He is able to turn our hearts and lives around as well as fix marriages. You are not alone. David loved pleasure more than Christ, his wife, and children. David never gave God full control of his life. He tried learning the Word of God but never came into the knowledge of truth. He wasn't able to find truth because he was arrogant, wicked, bitter, and prideful. David had no power with Christ, luke warm, not operating in Christ and no spiritual life. He needed to be loved by God and everything else would have worked out fine. Respect your marriage everyone, sin will be revealed, nevertheless what is done in secret or darkness will come to light. No matter how long it takes, it will come out. God sees all of us and what we do. There is no hiding spot that He can't see. Wendy could only pray for her husband, herself and their marriage. Again, try letting God love us all and watch the situation change for the better, in the relationship or marriage. Get down on your knees and pray for each other.

Showing Your Beauty in Christ

Once you accept Jesus Christ in your life, we become one with Him. We lay down our life, so Jesus may have full control of us and our situations. There is no better person who can handle, bad behavior or bad situations in our life. Jesus went to the cross for all our sins and we need to go to the cross with all our problems and issues. What a beautiful thing Jesus did, just for us. In Wendy's relationships and marriage, she was able to forgive because of God's love. In her marriage, she stayed in it because of the vows, even though they separated for some months. The situation was there for a reason, maybe to get both Wendy and her husbands' attention. If there was no problem, God wouldn't be there either. So sometime things happened because God has been trying to talk to us but got rejected. People miss what God is calling us to do because they wouldn't accept Him. God is love and beautiful for handling all kinds of bad circumstances and problems in our life.

God will never leave us nor forsake us, even in worst situations. While going through hardship and problems in marriage and relationship, watch your reaction. Are you still being gentle and kind? Or are you acting worse than you was before the problem got out of hand? When serving God, no matter what the situation looks like, showing the Lord's character nature is the best way to respond, to people. God put a person in your life or have people come to you, when you are at your worse. Jesus will not quit on us and He doesn't want us to give up on a loved one. He wants us to minister to their heart and let them know something good, can come out of difficult or bad situation. The meaner the person be, is because they need you to minister to their heart. While Wendy continued to deal with her husband and talk about Jesus, the more God's grace abides in her. The meaner the problem and the more difficult it gets, people really need you, some might do not want to admit to the truth. They allow their pride to stand in the way of their blessing. Situations always find a person out and show what is inside the heart. If you are serving and doing the will of God, do what the Bible says to do and don't make yourself look bad. Christ is love and beauty, if you are showing bad manners that is not

God. You might need, Him to search your heart and see if there is any wicked ways in you that is not of Him. All things (bad situation) are for our sake, so we can grow in Christ and mature. Wendy loved her husband, instead of focusing on the problems, she knew God wanted to use her, for His glory. Read—1 Corinthians 13 chapter, 2 Cor. 1:9, 4:8, 5:18, 4:15, Roman 5:20 and Proverb 3:5

Understanding Our Old Sin Nature

Once we come into the knowledge of old sin nature and understand why the marriage or relationship isn't going well, maybe you will want to change some things. Wendy wanted to do what was right and David still had the old sin nature ruling and reigning in his life. Sin has you lusting in the fresh, not knowing which way to turn. A person can become clueless to what their responsibilities are in the relationship or marriage. They have been hurt, let down and felt unwanted which make it harder for them to change their ways. Some have no idea, how to change the situation, or change for the better. We are tempted every day, at work, in the streets, at a friend's house, and at a mall etc. But it is up to us to turn away, walk away or say no thank you. Old sin nature will say, yes to thing they know they shouldn't allow to happen in their life. Some people don't realize most destruction is a test, from Satan, to mess up your happy home. There are others who are jealous of someone else's relationship or marriage because it isn't working out. Sleeping around and married, you have others who don't care if you are in a relationship. Satan will whisper in your ear it is ok to cheat on your loved one and say they will not find out but God sees everything. What is done in the dark, will come to light and be revealed. Watch out for the devil, he is a snake and does bite. He comes to steal, kill and destroy, every marriage, relationship, children, parents and families. (Proverb 10:12) hatred stir up strife, but love covers all sins. Forgive and love is what everyone needs, inside of them.

Old sin nature will have you stuck in an abusive marriage or relationship. Thinking there is no way out of the problem. Old sin nature, can make you have low self-esteem, fear of leaving the person and unwanted by someone else. When a person continues in their same old bad habits, doing the same thing over and over again and getting the same results. It make you feel alone and have you wanting someone to help heal the hurt. Have you giving yourself to things you wish not to have but do it anyway because of disappointments in your life. Old sin nature repeat itself without thinking about changing. We try to fill the wounded empty space because of the pain, anger, and pride. Looking for a good feeling in, all the wrong things, in all the wrong places. Not knowing God is our source of light and all we need. Sin can bring back old memories, make you be unfaithful, cheat, steal and lie. God want to break these bad habits and give us new habits. To get all that junk out of our system, so He can bless us with better things. He wants to fill us with true love, His agape kind of love which is powerful. God's love can remove all the old sin nature out of the way. When we believe, He will bless our soul. Mrs. Black had to let go of her old nature and trust God in her marriage. God love us all and will never leave us. We all have to make changes in our life some time or another and just trust the Word of God. Wendy had to continue to trust in Jesus Christ.

Healing the Marriage

When your marriage begins to fail and divorce is stepping in. You must really try to sit down with your spouse and communicate. Ask questions, do not fear or be afraid because it is time to speak up and stop holding everything inside of you. Remember without talking to one another, sharing feelings, letting each other know what's on the mind and without communicating there is no relationship. There are plenty of marriages and relationships like this and they last only a short period of time. Is this what we both want to happen or realize we both need help? First talk it over between the two of you. Express your feelings and what you would like from one another. Listen to your partner carefully and make some changes which would help the marriage get better. Try not to accuse the other person for their wrong because most of the time both are responsible for the problem. Let's heal our broken heart and make marriages last the way it should. Love one another, communicate, share the things you suppose to, and change the things that are destroying the children, spouse and family. (Matthew 15:18) but those things which proceed out of the mouth come forth from the heart, and they defile the man. 21 Century King James. Heal the marriage by speaking gentleness and kind words to each other. Find out what is the real problem, get to the root of the situation and go beyond your feelings and fix the marriage. Make a change and have proof that Jesus did it and will do it for everyone else.

Ways to Make the Marriage Work

There are ways to make marriages and relationships work. These are some ways, Mrs. Black had to do. The very best way is through the Blood of Jesus Christ and His agape kind of love. We have to believe in Jesus and the His word (the Bible), that is where our strength, deliverance, healing and help comes from. No other way. People can make us feel happy for a moment, feel good for a few minutes, and can bring pain to the heart. With Jesus, the Blood will set us free from past and present disappointment, bad marriage, bad relationship, headaches, and stress. His love will carry us through and you will be able to see the difference. First, but to always respect your husband or wife. The temptation today is much stronger, and we seem to fall into anything a man or woman say to us, if it sounds good. People fall for the kind words when the relationship or marriage is falling apart and they can't seem to find out how to fix what is broken. So instead of trying to make the marriage or relationship work, they add more problem to it and become more disrespectful to their mate. You got yourself in the marriage or relationship, now it is time to figure out a way to keep it strong and not make it worse. It is easy for people to get into something and hard to get out. God is there for us, all we have to do is accept His love, let Him in your heart, let Him lead us, guide us in the right direction and that is when you would be able to see the light. What God put together, never allow the devil to stir up confusion between the two and in the home. The devil comes to steal, tear down, break up, make miserable, kill, harden heart, put you to shame, upset the family and destroy. Believe the Word of God and He will make a way out of no way. Trust, believe, and have faith. Save the relationship and marriage and put Satan to shame, let the devil know, he tried but my God is much bigger and stronger than the devil.

The Marriage Looks Impossible

It might look impossible for a marriage to be fixed but with God all things are possible, to those who believe, in His put and keep Jesus Christ first in any and everything you do. Ask, Christ to show you, His ways and His love. We have to learn to love ourselves before we can love others. Show your love to your mate, even though they might not deserve it. This is how Jesus loves us, no matter what we have done wrong and in spite of our sins. His love never changes but people's love toward us changes daily. Show you care for each other, apologize, give hugs and kisses, do small things that make them smile, and always tell them you love them. Spend time alone together, go to a movie or watch movie at home, walking in a park, go food shopping together, walking in the mall and maybe go out to eat. Just being there together makes all the difference. (Ecclesiastes 3:1-8) everything has its time also, 11:10, 12:14. There are lots activities both parties can do without spending money, while enjoying life as one. Just like you did when you first met and you just wanted him or her. And now you have that person, if you marry them for life. Continue to build the relationship up, keep the body looking good, keep the fire burning and your other half happy, until death do you part, Amen.

What God Put Together

What God put together let no man, woman, child, friend, or family come in between. God made marriage for a life time for people to have families, to show love, to never depart great name. Wendy found out that no marriage or relationship is perfect and that is why it takes work. Just like when we go to work at a job. Some jobs a person has to be trained for and work hard at. Marriage takes work, it is for the rest of your life, to be with one person and a job some of us retire from jobs. On a job all your life a person had to put up with a lot of stuff, had to hung in there, only had a couple of years left, couldn't wait to retire but they made it work. Marriage is the same way, you have to spice the love up, do different things, travel for your honeymoon, show kindness, be gentle, caring, and be meek. There should be a time in your life when peace in the home should enter again. A place you enjoy coming home to, to see the wife, the man of the house, children, quietness, peaceful, joy, light and happiness. When the marriage looks impossible, call on Jesus, get on your knee daily, pray for God, to change you, obey God's Word, stay focused on the One who is able to keep us from falling and watch Him move on your behalf. God can do anything but fail and there is no one like Him. Think positive about the other person and keep praying for yourself and the mate. (Matthew 26:41)" watch and pray, that ye enter not into temptation. The spirit indeed is willing but the flesh is weak". 21 Century KJ Bible. What seems impossible, could become a miracle or testimony! It will help other people who, are going through the same problem, you had but with God in your life, everything starts turning around for the good. Learn to be patient, encourage yourself and your mate, forgive them for their wrongs, and be the bigger person to say "I really do love you." Let your spouse and others see that you have truly made up in your mind, to turn from sinful habits and turn to Jesus Christ. Prove it by the way you speak, think, act, the way you walk uprighteously and live according to the word of God.

Never Give in or give up

Sometimes we have to fight for what belongs to us. Once a couple got married, they became one. What is mine, is also yours (ours). We are no longer one apart but one together as a whole. Let go of hatred, unforgiving spirits, bitterness, anger, arrogance, and give it all to God in prayer daily. Forgive completely from the heart, just like God forgave us for all of our sins and wrong doings. Be patient, while waiting on the spouse, think about the good they have done in the relationship and never give up on them. Be a soldier, standing strong and tall. Give honor, praise, worship and glory to our Lord and Savior. When we magnify, glorify, and lift up the name of Jesus, it gives us strength and helps us to proceed in our faith. Help us to have confidence in the marriage. Use God's power and authority, to resist the devil and he should flee away from you. It keeps the devil away but don't give him a place in your life again once God removes him. Mrs. Black said, for her the Bible is her foundation to life, meaning use the Bible—your basic instruction before leaving the earth. The Bible is our weapon to fight off anything which is not of God and everything which is against, His word. Work together in your marriage, it is not always easy but if both persons truly care for one another and if you respect the vows you took, hang in there and make it happen. What do you have to lose? Stop thinking the grass is greener on the other side and work with what you have. (Ephesians 4:32) and be ye kind one to another, tender hearted, forgiving one another, even as God for Christ's sake hath. Never allow people in your marriage business but be kind and faithful toward each other. Marriage can be so romantic, caring and loving. It starts with having God agape kind of love; this love casts out fear and goes beyond and above, in order to keep the love strong. Why love someone else when your mate is at home, depressed and wondering where the marriage went out of control. Watch out for Satan, the devil is working all day long and so is Jesus. Never give up or give in; fix the marriage by giving and showing love.

IT Takes Two

If one party or person is trying hard to make the marriage or relationship work, it's not going to work. It takes both people to make a marriage work. When one person is pulling one way and the other another way that isn't going to work. If you are not married and this is going on you can get out of the relationship. But in a marriage before getting out, they must try to find ways to work it out and get on the same path of righteousness. Just like it takes two people to have a child. Your partner wants feedback from you and help with making decisions. Make future plans together. How to save and buy a home, pay off the cars, got out of debt, have a billing list of things that need to get paid off, budget lists, and see where the money is going. Do we have the important things in Life? Like life insurance, funds for the children in case some happens to the parents, 401k, or savings. Communication is very important so is trust. When the trust is broken always admit when you are wrong instead of harming the relationship more. Some men and women don't admit they're wrong and continue to do wrong. (Romans 12:17) recompense no man evil for evil. Provide things honest in the sight of all men. Most of us find it hard to forgive and that is why we need God in our life so we can move forward and not backward. No one wants to stay struck in the past, or to be arrogant, hurting, rude, holding on to hatred and carrying curses down to your children. Children (Matthew 19:19) honor thy father and mother; and thou shalt love thy neighbor as thyself. Parents also need to show love and spend time with the kids. Forgive now, stop putting it off because not everyone wakes up the next day, that day is not promised to anyone. Again, work together as one and be thankful for what you have and God will bless you.

Wendy had to keep her mind on God. Winning lost souls to our Lord and Savior Jesus Christ, was one of her goals. She understood that not all people know about Jesus, because she was one of them. She knew of Him but not enough to know what her purpose was while here on earth until years and years later. So, for the men women, young, old, marry, single, and person separated, who are holding onto unforgiving spirits, depression, bitterness, pain, suffering, and stress. There is help, and His name is Jesus Christ. Get rid of all these unforgiving spirits that are holding you back from, God's agape kind of love. The love that can heal, deliver and put hearts back together again. Satan enjoys messing with our mind and doesn't want to see, marriage work, doesn't like people to be happy and wants to keep all of us in bondage. We have a choice to make, free decision to choose what is right or wrong, to do the right thing or stay in bondage but it is up to us. Wendy has chosen to come out of the darkness and walk in the light. To help as many people as she can so they don't have to live in all that pain year after year and not knowing; Jesus is the way, the light, the truth, and life. He is able to help everyone, who comes to Him for help. He can take that heartache and turn it into joy. Wendy knew how it felt to be let down, and betrayed by a loved one who you trusted and truly loved. But she knew to return to Jesus, the one who has been keeping her all these years of her life.

When your mind is filled with disappointment, anger, jealousy, unforgiving and confusion, you can't think correctly. You feel weak, empty, blind, feel like death, and can't find your way. A part of you is missing and we think it is the one who has hurt us and caused the pain. But why so much hurt and pain if they love us? Because true love doesn't come from people and material things in the world but only from Heaven above, Jesus Christ. Avoid looking for people to make you feel good and make you happy but look to the hills where your help comes from. People will always let you down, harm you, make you feel bad and walk out of your life forever but not God. Relationships can leave you scarred for life, make you have low self-esteem, make you feel like no one wants you, and make you lose your mind.

Try not to stay in something that continues to hurt and cause you lots of pain. Stress can cause sickness, bring disease upon your body, have you on drugs, and doing thing that are not good for you. All because someone has hurt you, put a curse on you and scarred you for life. There is a way out and that is through the blood of Jesus who can wash away all sins. Put the past behind you, by repenting, accept Jesus into your life, believe in His Word, have faith, trust Him with all your heart and do His will. Most of us have experienced disappointment in life. You are not alone.

When the trust has been broken, follow your heart. If you fall down, get back up in the name of Jesus, call on that name. Pray about everything you do, pray for protection, pray every morning, all day, pray when you are driving, pray for the whole world, pray for answers, pray for direction, pray for God's will for your life and pray for God's will to be done on earth as it is in Heaven. Have an intimate relationship with the Heavenly Father, it helps us love each other. Do unto your spouse what you would want done to you. When discouragement comes, sing praise to the Lord, it gives you strength from day to day, changes the heart, gives you a humble heart, a peaceful heart and a forgiving heart which now can show love to many people. People who don't know God, need to see true belief and be followers of Christ the light shining through them, showing His love to all mankind. Believing souls are blessed souls. Why let others continue to take advantage of us? When God promises us many blessings and He will and is able to perform them. God wants us all to be made righteous in Christ. Get to know Him and see just how faithful, He is and you won't be disappointed. We trust other that we don't know and fall in love, so let's give Jesus a chance and see if we can fall in love with Him like we do with other strangers in this world. There is victory in the name of Jesus and every day we get to magnify, His name. Every day is a day of thanksgiving, God's been so good to us all. And every day He is blessing us. Amen.

A Mind Discipline

Wendy's mind had to be disciplined with the knowledge of Jesus Christ. To study the Bible, believe it, live it, have faith, share it and possess the truth in her heart. She had to concentrate on what God was speaking to her heart and mind, refuse to let anyone distract her from believing in the name of Jesus. She refuses to mix faith with what the world said, and listen to the spiritual side. The spiritual mind is food to her soul man and it helps discipline the mind, body and soul. As she meditates on the mind of Christ, her behavior begins to change and she was able to forgive everyone. Everyone has a call on their life and deserves to be forgiven by others. She admitted and confessed, her wrong doing and sin to Christ. This lady had a capacity to forgive because she understood the power and ability of God's love. God wants to anoint us with His power, the Holy Spirit. Once you become equipped with God's righteous, power and love than you can be set free from blind spots. Blind spots are areas in your life that are darkened by self and a person refuses to control their attitude, by not obeying the Word of God.

She had to control her blind spots by speaking happiness, joy, singing praise songs, worshipping Christ, and fellowshipping with believers in Christ. She spoke about her relationship with Jesus, she prayed and put on His character nature (whole armor of God). God is able to deliver all if we ask Him. Wendy was delivered from stress, sickness, old sin nature, bad decision making, being angry, and out of Satan's Kingdom. Once He cleanses our minds, then He is able to work in and through a mind which has been disciplined. Wendy realized, she was nothing without Jesus Christ and could do nothing. A disciplined mind helps a person focus more on God and what their purpose is while on this earth. She knew without God, it would have kept her repeating bad habits, stay away from the presence of God, be still weak minded and weak, with no power to fight the devil.

Trials and tests come to make us stronger, help us mature in the mind and take God's Word more seriously. Never play with God's Word or take it for granted. Sometimes God sends the people who have caused you pain, back in your life for a reason and that is to do the impossible and forgive. It shows a person true love, character and the nature of God. The world might not understand, how you were able to forgive someone because of your long suffering and no complaining but that only the true disciple of Christ can. Seeing a real true believer hurting, not complaining, and able to forgive shows God's love. Mrs. Black was that woman, a lady after God's own heart and wanting to be more loving like Him. See things through God's eyes and not your own. (Roman 7:18).

You will be able to see a mind discipline by God. The evidence inside of you will glow in the dark and light up like fireworks. Be on fire for our Lord and Savior, choose to forgive and let your light shine in this dark world. Be a blessing to many, by having a cheerful, loving and peaceful heart. Blessed is a man of whom the Lord shall not impute sin. (Roman 4:8). Wendy came into the knowledge that she just couldn't go to church, or obey the Bible, or service God, nor win lost souls, stay in her comfort zone, blame others for her pain and hold onto grudges. Some people were just like Wendy and some still are and refuse to change. Doing things their way and thinking it is right instead of doing things God's way. Only the things that are done for Jesus Christ will last, but things not of Jesus will not amount to anything at all. It His way or no way, we are either for Christ or Satan and it can't be both. You can't serve two masters. Let God discipline you and renew your mind. He doesn't show hatred, plot against, or hurt people's reputation and character. He only shows love and forgives all. Why stay vexation; we are to get rid of worry, jealousy, anger, revenge and bitterness. Don't withdraw from God but draw nearer to Him. You are not alone and all of us need to change some things in our life. And if you feel you don't need to change, keep on living and you will see that we all need God.

Love No Matter What

Wendy realized as long as she was on this earth, there was going to be times in her life that things weren't always going to be peaches and cream. The problems she experienced in her relationships and marriage, was a tremendous test. The hatred caused in her heart had to be turned around to love no matter what. She had to forgive in order to see the light God was trying to show her. That was a blessing from pain, fear, jealousy, an unforgiving spirit, and loss of the person she once was loved. The love had grown dark, cold, depressed, a heart full of sorrow, a worried mind and a body empty inside. Through it all, it led her to Jesus. She learned to trust in Jesus and depend upon His name. The disappointment, sadness, and struggle with loneliness showed Wendy that people will hurt you and leave you but not Jesus. He is there to the end and a real friend. Forgiving and just be able to say hello and talk to a person once it's over, makes you feel good because you are over them and don't want them back. But you can only do this with God's help and His agape love. The agape love of God, it loves everyone and no matter what a person has done to or for you.

Revenge was on her mind but thanks to God, Wendy thought about it before she acted. She couldn't keep making excuses and blaming the men in her life for her unhappiness because she could move on. She didn't have to put up with a person who lied, cheated and cause her pain. Once God brings you out of something, make sure you don't go back into the same mess again. She asks God to restore her again, fix it again and work out the problem. Always praise God until he shows up, give yourself a way to Him only, and make up your mind to follow Christ. When you sing, worship and praise the Lord, it helps you love others because you are building yourself up in Christ and his blood gives you strength from day to day. The blood will never lose its power, and it will wash away all your sins. Once you overcome confusion, face your battles, let go of grudges, and stop condemning people you will know it was God that brought you out. All Wendy could do was dance, dance all night and praise Him. So many times she tried things her way but the pain was still there and she knew that only God could heal and deliver her.

Wendy was down for so long but only Jesus can stop those tears, and there will be no more crying nights. There is a stronger love in this world and He can make a way out of no way. Being thirsty, hungry, and on fire for Jesus, He will show you how to love when you are hurt and down. Your praise, worship and fellowship with other believers brings fuel to the fire. Win souls to Jesus and praising Him bringing fuel to the fire. Angels in heaven rejoice when you win just one soul. It shows your relationship you have with Jesus because He is worthy to be praised. Wendy presents her life to Jesus, because He won't let her down, he won't break her heart and he won't let her fall, so she gives her life to Him. For His glory, Wendy would do anything just to see His face because we have victory in the name of Jesus. Everything about Him, is right, true, everlasting, real, amazing, and strengthens us from day to day. He's forgiving and loving. If you are one of His disciples, have His character nature and ways, obey Him, do what the Bible commands, Love one another and respect your parents, and hear his voice than you can say, I'm a child of God. Because his sheep, hear his voice and obey. Forgive and love, just as Jesus forgave and love us all.

Change people, place and things

Wendy wanted to change her life, how she wanted things, how she saw things and her thoughts. It was time to think about more important situations.

Fiction Stories—How To Forgive

Story #1—Cindy Raped

Cindy was raped by two men. She became pregnant and had a little girl. She knew children are a blessing and a gift, from God. Cindy was undecided, on whether to keep her daughter or give her up for adaptation. One Saturday morning, she woke up feeling depressed. It wasn't because Cindy had the baby but how would she explain to her child, once she got old enough to understand. On the other hand, she had time to think about it and just take very good care of her daughter. As time went by while rising the child they became close and the love was strong.

Cindy's daughter is grown now and she did ask about her dad. Cindy looked at her, she became glassy eyed and tears rolled down her face. She told the daughter, "I expected that question to pop up some day. I was raped by two men. I was angry at first, but my doctor told me not be depressed because I could lose the baby. The doctor, asked if Cindy wanted the child and she said, yes and that she didn't want to kill a human being. She explained, to her daughter, how she had to pray and lean on God to help her through the pregnancy and the rest of her life. The word she spoke to her child proved that Cindy was a strong woman, as well as forgiving those men for they knew not what they have done. Besides her mom could have gotten on drugs, killed herself or lost her mind. Instead, Cindy forgave, moved on with her life and raised a beautiful young lady. Her daughter, was so proud of her. They hugged one another as tears flowed with love and peace. Cindy stated she could not have make it without the Lord on her side. She wanted everyone to know it wasn't easy but if you want peace of mind, please forgive every person who may have wrong you and you will feel much better.

Story # 2—Shirley Taken From Behind

Shirley was on her way to the Bright Mall, to meet up with some friends. She parked her car on a side street, one block from the Mall. Shirley got out of the car and begin walking. A heavy set, light skinned man, approached her from behind with something pointing in her back. The man put a black bag over her face and push her, in his van and drove off. This man took her in a wooded area, far out in no man's land. There was a cabinet in the woods and he kept her there for 2 days and repeated beat and raped Shirley. She asked the male to please let her go and why was he doing this to her? He said, his mother's boyfriend had raped him for years and he never got help. Shirley said that she was sorry to hear that but what he was doing is wrong. Next the woman told him she know where he can get help from. He stated, no one can help me and never try to help me. She said, "Please will you let me help you and will you trust me."

Shirley begin telling him, about the Gospel of Jesus Christ and how He died on the cross for all our sins and how Jesus forgives us. The man said that he heard of the name Jesus but never went to church or no one explained Jesus to him the way she did. Shirley asked if she could pray for him and he answered yes! The man began to cry and she prayed and prayed for his deliverance. He accepted, Jesus as his Lord and Savior and let her go. He turned himself into the police and spent about 10 or 15 years in jail. He thanks, Shirley for the Word of God and was reading the Bible in jail and telling everyone in jail, his testimony and how he felt now. Shirley forgave him and there was no disease or harm to her body. She just thanked God that she was able to help another lost soul and now the man can see that there are good people out there and God is the answer to all of our problems. God is a healer and deliver. Shirley wants people to know that when you forgive and let go of hatred in your heart, a soul could be saved and be converted to Jesus Christ. Help people get to Christ and not run them away from His presence because we all need Jesus.

Story #3 A Mother of a Set of Twins

Sarah, a mother of a set of twins, who became hospitalized after being taken advantage of by one of her husband's best friends. Sarah's husband was out of town on a business trip for a week. Thursday evening the doorbell rang, it was Joshua, her husband's friend. The twins were at the grandmother's house and Sarah was straightening up the house some. Joshua came by to see, if Sarah and the kids were ok, also to see if they needed anything. She told him everything was ok and her husband should be home in three days. As Sarah was walking the man to the door and telling him thanks for coming by, Joshua turned and said, "I always liked you."

Sarah said, "But I love my husband very much and how could you say such a thing like that!"

He grabbed, her by the neck and headed upstairs to the middle bed room. Next, he threw her on the bed, ripping her clothes off, while Sarah was pleading for him not to touch her. Joshua refused to listen. She was a very attractive woman and he just had to have her. He took what belonged to his best friend, a person who trusted him. After he raped with her, he asked Sarah not to mention it to her husband and that he was sorry. Sarah was in shock, was crying, and couldn't believe Joshua was so cold. He left and Sarah immediately, called her husband.

Sarah's husband was so upset, he got on the next plane home. He told her to call the police and she did, just that.

The police came, wrote a complaint and later got the warrant for Joshua's arrest. He tried to lie and said that, Sarah came onto him. But they had evidence from the cameras in the house which you could hear every word and it showed what had happened. Sarah was in the hospital for months but her husband prayed daily for her recovery. He wanted to hurt Joshua but his wife told him God will take care of the situation and that they both needed to forgive Joshua.

They both forgave him but it was hard for them. But they knew, it had to be done because of the love they had for the Lord, dwelling inside them. They remember when the Lord forgave them for all of their sins and wrong doing. They learned in the Bible, God said, forgive everyone or He will not forgive you. Sarah's husband visited Joshua, to let him know what he really wanted to do to him but thanks be to God, the one who is able to keep us from falling. The husband was able to let him know they forgave him but never to come near them again. Joshua has been beaten about five times while in jail. Sarah is much better and is back at home with her loved ones Amen.

Story # 4 Paula and Walter

Paula had been with, Walter for ten years now and married for eight years. They had good times and were always together. When bad times came in the relationship they worked it out together. He' was a hardworking man, didn't miss work too often, unless he was really sick. He did bring, old baggage that wasn't dealt with from his past behavior because some people become obsessed with another. He was with another woman before Paula but didn't break the relationship off. He was still talking to the lady but only whenever Paula wasn't at home. Walter went over the woman's house two times in the beginning of him and Paula's relationship. He told the lady, this last time with her that he was with Paula. And he will not continue seeing her because it is not right. The girl was upset and that night she followed Walter to Paula's house. This person knew where Walter worked, so one day she went back to the house and Paula was home. She rang, the doorbell and Paula answered the door. Paula said, "Hello how can I help you?"

The lady said, "Walter is my boyfriend and we are still seeing each other."

Paula stated, "We are engaged and will be getting marry in about five months."

Paula called Walter while the woman was still there and he answered the phone. She told him, "Your lady friend stopped over here today and told me that you are her man."

Walter said, "I told her it was over long time ago and that I will deal with my responsibility with the right attitude, when I get off work."

When Walter got off work, he went home, got Paula and went over to talk to the lady. Paula said, "Men don't like to talk when they do wrong because they will get twisted up in more lies."

She knew that some men also get mad when their mate keeps asking questions because they are lying. Walter on the other hand, was telling the truth. He even took Paula with him to clear the problem up. The woman received, the message and Walter never had to worry about her again. He told Paula, that he was very sorry for her coming over to their home and would she forgive him. She said, yes I forgive you and they hugged and kissed. Walter knew, his darkness had been over and he was really trying to be faithful to that one woman. That little problem almost cost him, his soon to be wife. Him and Paula, pray together and their focus is on Jesus. With them having a relationship with GOD, it helped mend the relationship and Paula was glad she was serving GOD, because that is what brought her through all her other hurt and pain. She realized, she belong to GOD, she wasn't going to give place to the devil, and allow him to destroy her relationship. Paula learned, never to look to the world or people, for your happiness. Measure your happiness by your call from JESUS CHRIST. Paula had to remember, her happiness doesn't come from other people, not family, friends, spouses, boyfriends but true happiness only comes from Jesus Christ. The couple did get married and had three children. They lived a pretty good life, thanks to Jesus Christ.

Always keep GOD's Spirit, first in your life, learn to forgive and mature. What GOD put together let no one tear it apart. Be strong in JESUS, stand in your authority and take back everything that belongs to you. Because everything and everyone has to vanish from this earth, we are only here on earth just temporary. Only thing that will stand forever is the Word of GOD. Paula said, in this life on earth, we are here to serve GOD, reveal GOD and get His gospel out to lost souls. Love your spouse, show honor to each other, cherish each moment, spend time together, show you truly care and always speak in love. None of us know the time or hour when we may leave this earth. Make sure you are in right standing with GOD call for your lives. He's the answer, will guide us in the right direction so we can be on the correct pathway to Him. AMEN.

Story # 5 Thomas Love for His Kids

Thomas had four children at a very young age, right after he had finished school. He started dating the first young lady and later began talking to another lady. Karen was the first woman and was pregnant by Thomas. Karen was getting ready to graduate from the 12th grade and was going to her prom. She went to her prom with a guy friend while she was pregnant but not the child's father to be. Later when Karen found out, he was fooling around, she broke the relationship off. Thomas had three other kids after the break up. Karen and Thomas were very good friends and their child loved both of them very much. She doesn't try to keep the child away from Thomas, just because they are not together. He apologized to Karen and she forgave him. Karen always showed him God's agape kind of love. On the other hand, he has three other baby's mothers who, try to keep the children away from Thomas. He's a man who doesn't have much but enjoys spending time with his children and loves them all the same. He tried to get all the kids together because he wanted them to have a good relationship. The kids love each other, call each other, and all the mothers sometime take the kids to either mother's house, so the kids can spend time together.

Thomas thanks God that his children are able to know each other and spend time together. The other women are not as close as Thomas and Karen but the kids being together is what matters the most. And the ladies are all mature enough to respect one another and their child. Thomas had a couple of girlfriends later, who didn't want to accept all his children by different women. Thomas never told them all the kids were by different ladies. So, he told them, if you can't accept his kids than they can't be with him because his children come first. Thomas stated, I made these kids and might not have much but spending time together is number one, to showing love and that you care. Thomas said that the kids need both parents and it hurt him to his heart when he can't see or be with his children.

If you are in a relationship or marriage and you know God, make sure you get all your children together and spend time with them. They need to know their brothers and sisters as well as their mom and dad. If you are going through something with a spouse, communicate with the person, wife or husband. Men be the head of your household and get your family in order. Take back everything the devil has stolen from you and go to God in prayer. Why continue to be that man crying in the dark, giving place to the devil, letting Satan continue to have control over the family. The devil comes to destroy, kill, and keep us depressed. Hasn't Satan done enough by trying to keep everyone down and in the pit. Men of God, what's taking so long; children are crying out for your love. What is God telling you to do? Thomas wants to say never disown your children, take a stand and let all the children be together. God knows everyone's heart and if you are doing His will or not. Showing love to all of your kids and leaving none out. You are not alone but God gives us plenty of time to get things in order and we are running out of time. You are all in my prayers but fix the problem with your Lord and Savior help.

Story # 6 Keep the Love Strong

There were two brothers who lived with their grandmother. Their mother passed away in a car accident and their dad was married but lived far away. They hadn't seen their dad in over 28 years. They did talk to him in the early part of their life but somehow they lost contact. As the years went by, one of the boys got real sick and needed some blood. No one had a match for the boy, so they had to start searching for their father. Time was running out and the doctor gave the male one month. They had a small family and the only one living was the great aunt and she lived far away. They did get in touch with her and she knew where the father was living. She gave the son the number and he called his father. This brother had two more weeks to go. The dad answered the phone and was glad that they had called. But the father was also very ill and was unable to give blood because of his illness. They both began to cry over the phone. The father was so sorry that he couldn't help and hadn't spent any time with the boys at all.

The father knew the Lord Jesus Christ and he attended church services. The boys also served Jesus Christ and attended church. They talked a little and all they could do is pray for both the son and dad's health. They prayed and prayed. The son told his dad that he will call back to check on him and that he was going back to the hospital to check on his brother. There was one more week left for the brother to live.

He was very weak and pale. The brother, church family and friends, continued praying and for their father as well. Three days were left when the doctors got a match and right away they began surgery. Prayer was still going on for both men. Six hours went by and the doctor came out and said that he was going to be alright. Once the brother got well enough to walk, both boys flew to go see their dad.

The father was in and out of the hospital and was unable to walk. They went to his house and the wife answered the door. She invited them in and took the young men to their dad's bedroom. He was so surprised to see them. They hugged and hugged each other as tears rolled down their eyes. They all were sorry that it took a long time for them to seek and find one another. The dad told them that the doctor said, he had a 50/50 chance to live. They begin to pray and stated to their dad, they are not leaving him and they will stay with him until they see what is going to happen.

A month went by and now it is time for his surgery. The wife was kind and showed her love toward the gentlemen (her husband's sons). The sons, thought the father's wife had a nice caring attitude toward them and their dad. It took hours for the surgery but thanks be to everyone's powerful prayers, faith, the believers in Christ's word, the support of his sons and God's power. He made it through all the pain and suffering. Him and his sons, spent the rest of their lives together. That was one of the best thing, that happen to them all and the wife, also enjoyed their company. Like what was mention before in the book, things happen for a reason and bad situations, can be turned around for the good. Situations can get people's attention because we can't see or don't understand. But God is calling us all to the cross, to get thing right and in order before His return, here on earth. You are not alone and it is never too later, just do it now and stop putting it off. They love their dad no matter what and they prove God's love because He is all love and beautiful. Thank you, Jesus. What a testimony, two in one Amen?

Story # 7– Refuse to Forgive

Kevin and Gary were best friends, for about 20 years now. Kevin had one of the prettiest girl in the neighborhood. All the guys liked her but Kevin ended up with her. His girlfriend's name was Catherine, nice smile, soft voice and a petite figure. Gary had a house warming party since he had just moved into a house. The rent was affordable and he was buying it. Most of the people were there at Gary's house but Kevin left his gift in the house, so he went home to get it. He told, Catherine he would be right back unless she wanted to come with him. She decided to stay there and wait. Gary did something, he never did before and that was hit on one of Kevin's girlfriends. This is his best friend's lady, she was nice looking and Gary said some things that weren't true about Kevin. Gary was getting fresh with her and said Kevin had other lady friend and he was using her for one thing."

Most people wouldn't tell if their boyfriend or girlfriend hit on them and that is because they want that person anyway too. But Catherine was mad and couldn't believe Gary said what he said to her about her man. When Kevin got back, she didn't waste any time and pulled him to the side and repeated everything Gary told her. Kevin was so upset, he wanted to fight but his girlfriend explained to him that it is not worth it. They gave Gary the gift and told him he was wrong. Kevin hasn't talked to Gary for three years but Gary was calling and going to Kevin's house to apologize. A few times he even left Kevin a letter in the mailbox, stating he was sorry. Kevin, Catherine and Gary all went to the same church sometimes. Kevin knew, he had to forgive him and let the past go and plus he missed his buddy. The two men were close friend and had so many good times together. One Sunday, Kevin and Catherine went to church, and the Pastor spoke to his heart about forgive others. Gary was in church also that day, he still kept going to church too and didn't let anything stop him from Christ.

After church was over Kevin, walked over to Gary and said, "I forgive you."

Gary promised it would never happen again and he was sorry. They started talking again and did some things together but not as much. Kevin made sure that he didn't get too close to his lady or was alone with her. God can and will change a mess into a blessing. He will give you a testimony and sometime God is testing you. It's how you react to different problems and are you doing what God's word says to do? We are living in Satan's Kingdom or God's Kingdom. We all have a choice to make and with Christ all things are possible. Forgive is the answer to peace and joy.

Story # 8—Left Without Answers

Angelica never had the chance to experience a real life with her dad. She said it truly hurts, make a person feel unwanted, and what did a child do to deserve this kind of treatment from a father. She always wondered does my father love me or does he just say it to make me feel good. Because he sure doesn't show it. It seems like this hole in her heart is getting bigger and bigger, from all the lies, the betrayal and all the pain he has caused. Angelica just can't take it anymore and felt let down by the man who means the most to her, in her life. While gazing in the mirror at herself, she wondered what do I mean to him? Is she just a child that doesn't matter anymore since she has grown up? Angelica feels that she needs just as much attention as any of his other children that he had in his new marriage.

She stared out the window, and asked God, "Do I deserve to be treated like this, to be the last on my father's list? I was here first before any of the other children, and daughters need to talk to their dad sometime, just like we talked to our mom. Does a father not know that his child has needs too and he is a big part of the daughter's life?"

This young lady found herself thinking about this often and sometimes cried herself to sleep just thinking about him. She never told her mom that this is how she felt about her father. Thoughts came to the child's mind, like does he claim me anymore? If he doesn't want to claim me, why didn't he tell me and why did he give me money in my younger days? Money is always a plus but does he feel sorry for me? Money can't heal a relationship or buy real true love but spending time together means a lot and can heal a person's heart. Angelica feels if he can give her money, he can show her love. She also wondered how often does he think about her and what happened to their relationship? Angelica thinks about what could've been, what should have been, what will never be but the main thing she think about most is does he love her!

Angelica loved her dad but wished she could have told him how she felt before he had passed away. Men and women love your children, never stop loving them, diligently show you care and please spend some of your time with them. Life is short, time doesn't wait on anyone and the next day is not promised to anyone. We are only on this earth for a short period of time, so enjoy your loved ones. It really hurts the kids after a break up, separation or divorce in relationships between the two parents. Parents are critical in a child's life especially the father, he is to be the role model because he is head of the household. He is to cherish, nourish and show love to his wife also show love to all his children. There are plenty of children hurting but God is there for all of us. You are not the only one who experienced life without a father. If your parents are still living and you find it hard to forgive them for not being in your life the whole time, please forgive them. There are plenty of parents who weren't there, but some children had it worse than you have. It's not too late, go to the person and forgive. When Jesus Christ is really dwelling on the inside of you, you will do what, His word teaches you to do. No matter what and God will do the rest. You are not alone.

Story # 9—Forgive Not

Mary had one best friend named Kelly. They went to elementary school together, all the way up to college. They were like sisters, sometimes dressed alike, went out to eat, party together, went to movies and went on date with guys etc. The two ladies were very close. They went out on a double date on a Saturday summer evening with two handsome guys. They were gentlemen, polite, kind and respectful. The evening went well and they all hooked up a few more times. Mary and Kelly weren't hanging out together like they used to because both relationship became serious with both men. But the ladies still called each other and went out sometimes, not often. About 5 years later Mary started having problems in her relationship and wasn't sure if her man was having an affair or cheating. She also realized that Kelly kept a distance from her and was slacking up on their friendship.

What had happened was Kelly broke up with her male friend about two years ago and was sleeping with Mary's man. Kelly had gone out one night to have a drink because she was depressed. Her man had been sleeping around and got a girl pregnant and Kelly was hurt. So that is how their relationship ended. In the meantime, Kelly was out drinking and had gotten drunk. Mary's man happened to be at that club with a few of his other male friends. He hadn't seen Kelly in about four month but Mary was still talking to her. She did tell

Mary, that her relationship wasn't going well after the third year but never told her when they broke up for good. Kelly was drunk. Mary's male friend went to speak to Kelly and saw that she was going to need a ride home. Kelly was trying to dance and fell on the dance floor. Mary's man helped her up and asked her if she needed a ride home because she shouldn't drive like that. So, he took her home and made sure she got into her bed. Kelly pulled Jim to her and kissed him. He was drinking but wasn't high like Kelly.

Kelly begin to come on to him and said she won't tell Mary if he wouldn't tell. She began taking off her clothes and telling him to take his clothes off. He said, he loved Mary and didn't want to lose her. He started walking away and said he had to go, when all a sudden Kelly come out the room butt naked and he fell for the devil's trick. From this point on he was sleeping with Mary and Kelly. Mary could tell something was wrong and the feeling wasn't right. Mary asked Jim if there was something he needed to tell her, he said no. Jim start coming in late and making excuses and Kelly was acting strange. Mary was trying to put two and two together but hoping it wasn't not true.

It was a Tuesday night when Mary went to Jim's job and waited outside. He got in his car and called Mary saying he would be a little late. He didn't know she was looking right at him while he was lying. Jim drove off and Mary followed him. He went to Kelly's house. Mary was hurt and couldn't understand why her long years of friendship, and best friend could be so cold hearted. Mary sat in the car for about twenty minutes, next she got out of the car and knocked on the door.

Kelly answered the door with a towel around her and Jim was at the top of the steps, asking who was at the door. They were taking a shower together; the two were busted and couldn't say a word. Kelly laid them out and left. She put Jim's clothes out of the house and didn't speak to Kelly for over five years.

Kelly ended up not being with Jim because he cheated on her. So that meant that Kelly had messed up a good long friendship between her and Mary over a man. Kelly and Jim only lasted two years. Kelly did try many times to say she was sorry and ask Mary to forgive her but Mary just couldn't do it right away. Kelly never stopped trying to be friends with Mary; she wrote Mary a nice long letter. The letter stated, how she was sorry and their friendship meant more than just some man. It took Mary years but after six years she forgave Kelly and they are friends again because they are like sisters. But that never happened again and neither of the girls drink any more. Jim is out of the picture and the friendship which they call each other sisters is doing well. Thanks to God. We live and you learn and it is all about how we handle the different situations. Both girls are now going to church with the family and plan to be married before having an imitate relationship with another man. Doing things God's way and in the right order. Amen.

Story # 10–Why Not Me

Mr. Wesley and Tammy were together for over thirty years but married for twenty seven years. They have seven children together. Tammy's mother had twelve kids and most of their family members have plenty of children. The family is large. Wesley was overweight and so was his wife Tammy. They were never that big until after having all the children. Tammy had to cook more and her and her husband were also eating more. They loved each other very much, loved all of their kids, were sweetheart lovers from school, and been together since school. They are older now in their late fifties and the wife worked night shift and the husband worked day shift. Tammy worked at an exercise spa. One Monday evening, Mr. Right came in and asked Tammy why she didn't exercise. She said, she was thinking about it because she needed to.

That Friday, it was slow in the spa and Mr. Right came in and asked Tammy to come work out. She did have her exercise outfit so she joined him. They were exercising and talking. They started working out together more often and Tammy started losing weight. She was looking good, after about seven month and Mr. Right told her, I knew you could do it and that she looks great. The two started liking each other.

Mr. Wesley also told her, she looked very nice. Her husband asked," Have you been working out?"

She said, yes. She was down to about 200 pounds and her husband was about 375. Mr. Right was about 160 pounds. Tammy and Mr. Right started having an affair and Tammy started having less sex with her husband. It has been going on for four months now; Tammy was acting weird with Wesley. Wesley wanted to know, why she stopped having feelings for him because she was acting different. She would cook, but stopped kissing Wesley, she stopped saying I love you, no hugs when she came home from work and not much communication anymore. Wesley asked if Tammy was having an affair, she said no.

He said, "Something is going on, since you lost weight. You act like you don't love me anymore."

She told Wesley, he needed to lose weight. He told her, he wouldn't mind losing weight but why didn't she tell him when she started because he could have worked out with her.

Tammy didn't respond. So, on Tuesday, Wesley went up to the spa to workout. As he walked in the door Tammy was in the back against the wall hugging and kissing Mr. Right. Wesley walked back there and asked how long has this been going on? Mr. Right said for four months.

Mr. Wesley told Mr. Right that Tammy was his wife and he can't have her. Mr. Right said, Tammy never said she was married and that he was sorry for messing with his wife. Mr. Right asked Tammy why did she do that to her husband? She said because he was the only man she been with all her life and once she lost weight she felt too good for him. Mr. Right told her to never let a good man go because you think the grass is greener on the other side. Mr. Right was single with no children and he respected the marriage and told Tammy he will no longer see her. He told Wesley they never slept together just hugged and kissed a few times. He told Wesley again, he was very sorry and would he please forgive him. Mr. Right never went back to that spa again. Mr. Right was a good man because most men don't care and will still sleep with your wife or lady. Wesley forgave the man and never saw him again. Wesley went home and waited for Tammy to come home. They had a long talk about what she did. She said, she was sorry and can he forgive her because that was the devil in her.

Tammy knew that it was God on her side because her husband could have left her. Mr. Wesley did go to church sometimes and was a very good husband and a good father to his children. He really loved Tammy and she loved him. See, sometimes the devil puts things in the way to hinder your marriage or break it up. But with God in the middle, you have a much better chance to handle the situation rather than fighting and leaving your loved one. Satan knows your weak spots and he will try you. The couple is exercising together and both are looking good and the marriage is so much better. Never lose weight and forget your spouse because they were always there for you. Don't let the devil distract you and make you lose the next best thing that ever happened to you. Make God your number one, first best thing in your life. There are problems that draw you to Jesus Christ. Amen. God is good.

Story # 11 – Wrong Pastor

Mrs. Gail loved her husband. He was a Pastor at Mount Church in Richmond, Virginia. They had no children yet. Been married for seven years, enjoyed tennis, soft ball and baseball. They met when Gail was trying to ride the horse and he was the one helping control the horse in case they get out of control. They had their disagreements, ups and downs but nothing too serious. Pastor Skip was faithful until one night, one of the member at the church called him and wanted to talk about a problem. It was about her son; the lady's son was getting into a lot of trouble and hanging with the wrong crowd. Pastor Skip told her to meet him Saturday morning at the church so they could talk.

This lady had problems in her marriage also. When she got to the church, she had on a short dress and the top low cut where you can see her breasts. She began telling the story about her son and Pastor gave her advice on what to do. Pastor told her she should have brought him with her. It didn't take long but when it was time to leave, Mrs. Bell try to get fresh with the Pastor. Pastor Skip told her she had the wrong man and he was all for Jesus Christ. He told her, the next time she would be talking to someone else in the church if she needed advice and there will be more than one person in the room to help her. Pastor forgave her but stayed away from that one on one with a lady. Pastors are not to ever be with any lady members of the church alone. No women. The devil will get you trapped up and try to hang you if, you let him. Be careful of the things you do, who you follow, how you pick your friends and watch where you go. People are watching your every move. Mrs. Bell felt so bad she never went back to that church because she was wrong.

Story # 12—Forgive and Show Love

Ruth was from the old school, she had three children. Two different children's fathers, two by one man and one by the other. She lived in a small town and there was only a few jobs in walking distance from her house. She was a single mom and worked all her life. Her personality was warm, caring, loving and she truly loved all her kids. She never hardly complained about anything, she worked and did her best to care for the kids. The children's father never paid child support or gave her money for them. Only one of the fathers came around to see his kids and sometime got all three children even though one wasn't his. As the kids got in a higher grade in school, they found work and brought their own belongs so their mom didn't have to do it. Their mom never mentioned the father unless the children asked about them and she never put the men down or spoke negative about them. The lady showed no kind of hatred toward the kid's dad, held no grudges, no anger, no bitterness, and didn't care to be with either one of them. Why waste your time being upset over something you have no control over, when you can move forward and do better. Please find ways to love, forgive and make peace with all men. Read—Romans 12:18-21. You all are in my prayers.

Story # 13 Unforgiving Spouses but with God

There was a couple who lived on top of a hill, in Green Top Village. They had three children and was married for 15 years. Bobby was the husband and Nancy was the wife. They did plenty of traveling together and with the children. This was a happy family but they weren't followers of Jesus Christ. They were content with each other and the things they did together. They have heard about Jesus but just didn't go to church and refuse to read the Bible. Nancy started hanging out with some of her neighborhood lady friends and drinking. They would go out twice a month on Saturday night. Bobby would stay home with the kids while she enjoyed herself because he trusted his wife. Nancy started drinking a little heavy and at home. She never drank wine or beer in the house. One Friday the 13th, Nancy went out with a group of women on her job, to a nice house party. She got so drunk and was acting very hot. Tony was there and he had started dancing with Nancy. She was all over him and touching him in places on his body that she shouldn't. Tony whispered something in her ear and she said ok. They both left the dance floor and ended up in one of the bedrooms. Nancy took her clothes off and so did Tony. The next day she couldn't remember what happened that Friday the 13th. She had a hangover and was sick.

Bobby had wanted to have sex that night but she had fallen asleep. When he touched her down below, and sniffed, it smelled fishy. The next morning Bobby asked Nancy if she made love to someone but she said no and couldn't remember. Tony had recorded it on Nancy's phone, what they had done that night. Later that evening, Nancy was still sick and Bobby looked through her phone and what he saw was shocking. He couldn't believe his eyes. He showed it to his wife and she was hurt. She also could tell, she was drunk. Bobby told her after their daughter's graduation from 12th grade, in June that he was leaving and it was over between the two. She told him she was sorry and please forgive her. He was so mad, after graduation day, Bobby left but stayed in touch with kids. It took years for Bobby to forgive Nancy. She stopped drinking and going out, started seeing a counselor and wanted her husband back. Three years later, Bobby forgave his wife and started going to counseling with her. They started seeking answers which only God could give them. By going to church, trusting God for help, leaning on Him for direction and healing. That is how they made their marriage work and their love to grow even stronger. God was missing in their life but they have Him now. They are dating all over again and trusting God, that the marriage would be much better with Him in it.

Story # 14— It Is Over

Pam said, she knew she should have never married Dwayne! He never liked paying bills, gave her no money, she would pay all the bills. He would get high, never help clean up and refuse to watch the children. No matter where they went, Dwayne found something to pick on Pam about and the arguments began. It got to the point years later that the two couldn't stand to be around each other. They both were messing around on each other in the marriage with no direction from God and no church service in their life. The couple was confused and got married for all the wrong reason. Pam said, that was the biggest mistake a person can do, get married because everyone else is doing it, to look good for a moment, to say you have a wife or husband, and knowing you really don't care for the person like they care for you.

It got so bad Dwayne moved out and got his own place. He was still messing around and Pam too. Dwayne got Shera pregnant with twin girls but still wanted to be with his wife also. But when Pam found out Shera had the babies, she filed for a divorce. They got their divorce and are not speaking to each other. They never forgave each other and either one is looking for God for help or directions. Some people don't take their vows seriously and think marriage is a fashion show or a dress up day. Marriage is to death do you part, it is forever and not a joke or game. Do things in the name of Jesus and in His way only. That way your marriage will have a better chance to last. You are not alone.

Story # 15 – What I Put Up With

Beth is an older lady, and is dating a man fifteen years younger than her. She does attend church and knows about God but doesn't truly know Him and Nelson doesn't truly know God neither. If Nelson did, he wouldn't do what he did to Beth. She had been with men who never treated her right. Now she is with Nelson a man who goes to church but is very disrespectful behind closed doors. Beth hadn't had a man for over twenty years after her last male friend, who was disrespectful to her. Nelson came in her life and knocked her off her feet. She was so in love with him. He was nice at first to Beth until, she told him how she was treated by other men and people. Once he saw how he could get away with using her, scaring her, hitting on her, disrespecting her in front of her friends and talk to her like trash he knew he had a dummy. He knew this lady can't walk too good and doesn't speak up for herself. Nelson took advantage of her because she was very caring, loving and would do anything for her man. Beth let Nelson treat her any kind of way and he even stopped her from going to church. That is where her strength come from but she was so weak and scared to be alone or without a man. She just put up with this sick man while she continued to be miserable and a prisoner in her own house. He doesn't do things with her, not on her birthday, Mother's day, Christmas, Thanksgiving and he don't help pay bills. "Who wants a person like this?" Beth said. How can she get out of this relationship when she knows she is a weak person? A person who is trying to get you to your grave early. Using you for every little thing you have.

Beth had her own house and two cars. Nelson was always driving one of her vehicles. He had his own place but stayed with her, took her car and stayed out whenever he felt like it. She better not ask where he been because Nelson will lay her out and hit her. Beth would sit in the house and cry, not knowing where Nelson was for days with her car. He thinks the car is his but it is what you allow a person to do to you. She is afraid to take it away from him and kick him out of her house. She took her car away from him a few times and it almost killed him. He got so sick one time, when she took her car and he ended up in the hospital. She didn't go see him and Nelson was in there for two weeks. When he got out of the hospital, he went over to her house begging her to let him in. She felt sorry for him and took him back in. Nelson came into this woman's life to steal, kill, and destroy her and she's so in love that it blinded her eyes. Do you see how we can be a fool for people who treat you wrong? Beth knows about God but refuses to go back to her helper. Because she knows, she is sinning anyway and getting dogged out by the devil. She forgives this man all the time, still does good by him but she is hurting on the inside. She is not the only woman who puts up with men like this. These men, who Beth calls, boys get away with murder and a lady still takes them back, no matter how many times they break their heart. They love them even more. God sees everything, by Nelson going to church, hurting Beth and playing with the word of God, he will reap what he sows. He may think he is getting away with treating Beth bad but God has something for him.

Beth needs to wake up, get her first true love back which is Jesus and let God search her heart. It is time for her to put her foot down and take back what the devil has stolen from her. Which is her Lord and Savior Jesus Christ, the word of God which has power, her peace, joy, soul, body, mind, happiness and peaceful home. She has given it all to Nelson and he is destroying her. The devil put Nelson in her path of righteousness to stop her from doing the Will of the Father and to keep her struck in bondage. Beth has to break those chains off of her and get out of that dark hole. Pick up that cross and move to victory in the name of Christ Jesus. Beth said, this is what she put up with and she allowed it so Nelson will continue until Beth stopped it. This is crazy, crazy love, something you can't define. Ladies you don't have to put up with this, especially if you are not married. It takes a fool to learn that love don't love nobody. Take your power back and joy. Be alone and spend time with Jesus, the one who does love you beyond your faults.

Encouraging Words

PRAY, FORGIVE AND SHOW love. Why do we allow the enemy to get away with what they do? Satan always tests the righteous people as well as the ungodly people. How many of us believe in the Bible and God's Word? The more you get to know Him, the more you will be able to trust Him and gain strength. He is alive and real to my soul. The best marriage is for you to live in God and glorify Him, don't try to change your spouse but pray for them and continue to show love. I understand when you are hurting, you might not want to pray and show love but trust God. Die to yourself daily and live for God. It will help Him to carry your sins away forever and help you become a better person. It helps to us deal with any situation without hurting people. Do everything in the name of Jesus Christ. Our walk with God, is so important to others. He is the answer. People see the cross through us, we are the light, life and salt of the world.

Some people have a Christian life but not a Spiritual Christian life, that doesn't do a thing for spiritual life. They have a different life, leading to their own understanding, make wrong decisions and have wrong souls. Fulfilling the lust of the fresh, that old sin nature still on the inside of them. They damage their own mind and are unhappy. John 17:3—Remember Eternal Life, we are on this earth only to know the only true God. That's the only reason and obey. Build a strong relationship with God, so you can be convert or change and make Godly decisions. You can think clearly and have a peace of mind. Knowledge always produces fruit, it forgives and show love. When we put our trust in Jesus and stay under the shadow of His wings something begins to change. The only way the world gets to see Jesus Christ is seeing a true believer suffering well and not complaining. Will you trust Him, believe on the word, have faith and let Him guide you? When you show yourself approve by the way you live and it is pleasing to God, a change will soon take place. Matthew 3:8, Prove by the way you live that you have really turned from your sins and turned to God. Galatians 5:16-23 will also teach you how to make a difference in your life. I pray everyone who read this book be bless.

Final Words

I PRAY THAT THIS book helps each person who reads it. This is a start to get us on the right path to peace and victory. I hope you all enjoy the stories and find them helpful. Most of the stories show that love never fails. Love and forgiving is very powerful and shows God's real character and nature and His ways in a person. It releases us from destruction, pain and unhealed issues. Use the weapons GOD gave you, His agape love and the Bible which is our Basic Instruction before Leaving the Earth. Love people unconditional and no matter what happen to you and in your life. God's sheep hear his voice and obey.

Learn to forgive, love, be kind, gentle, meek, and longsuffering. Say what's on your mind in a nice way and go to the person alone. Show you really care for your husband, wife, children, family, friends and love your neighbor. Try not to destroy, condemn and hurt people but tell them the truth in love. Let GOD correct them and you continue to love them. True happiness only come from JESUS CHRIST, and not people. We all have a need for GOD, when we are hurting, go at His feet in prayer.

Build yourself up by listening to a Pastor, Teacher, read scriptures in the Bible, take Bible classes, attend Bible College, be filled with the Lord's Spirit, walk in wisdom, get knowledge, understanding and a revelation of JESUS CHRIST. Make peace and forgive, never, never, give up. Put away sin nature, bitterness, pride, unforgiving spirit, jealousy, drunkenness, discord, thanklessness, confusion, curses, doubt and depression in your heart. Draw nearer to JESUS CHRIST and ask Him to bring complete healing to you and the person you have something against. Find ways to forgive and make things work. Remember GOD chastises and disciplines in order for us to get right with Him. Divine discipline is for the believer who is out of fellowship with GOD. All believers must learn how to respond to GOD. You are not alone, let's pray for each other, stay in the word, read often, meditate and be blessed. The best is yet to come. You are all in my prayers. GOD wants to bless us all. AMEN.

Author,

Printed in the United States
By Bookmasters